AMERICAN INDIAN CONTRIBUTIONS TO THE WORLD

Science and Technology

EMORY DEAN KEOKE

KAY MARIE PORTERFIELD

CHELSEA HOUSE
PUBLISHERS
An imprint of Infobase Publishing

Science and Technology

Maps on pages 39, 126–136 © 2005 by Carl Waldman
Maps on pages 58, 74, 137–138 © 2005 by Infobase Publishing

Chelsea House
An imprint of Infobase Publishing
132 West 31st Street
New York NY 10001

ISBN-10: 0-8160-5397-9
ISBN-13: 978-0-8160-5397-1

Library of Congress Cataloging-in-Publication Data
Keoke, Emory Dean.
    American Indian contributions to the world. Science and Technology / Emory Dean
Keoke, Kay Marie Porterfield.
        p. cm.
    Includes bibliographical references and index.
    ISBN 0-8160-5397-9
    1. Indians—Science. 2. Indians—Mathematics. 3. Indian astronomy. 4. Indian metal-
work. 5. Inventions. 6. Technological innovations. I. Title: Science and technology.
II. Porterfield, Kay Marie. III. Title.
E59.S35K46 2005
500' .89'97—dc22   2004010986

Text design by Erika K. Arroyo
Cover design by Cathy Rincon
Maps by Sholto Ainslie

Printed in the United States of America

VB FOF 10 9 8 7 6 5 4 3 2

This book is printed on acid-free paper.

For our grandchildren:
Jason Keoke, Gwendolyn Z. McPherson,
Matthew Geboe, Jr., and Jonathan Ward McPherson;
for future generations;
and in memory of Merrill W. Bowen, Jr.

✄ *Note on Photos* ✄

Many of the illustrations and photographs used in this book are old, historical images. The quality of the prints is not always up to current standards because in many cases the originals are from old or poor quality negatives or the originals are damaged. The content of the illustrations, however, made their inclusion important despite problems in reproduction.

CONTENTS

AUTHORS' NOTE

At least 800 unique tribes, or bands, of Indian people lived in the Americas at the time Europeans first arrived there in 1492. A tribe is a community or group of families who share the same culture, or way of living. The things that make up a culture can range from clothing and housing styles to ways of singing or praying. They include how people make and decorate the objects that they use in their daily lives. Tribal members speak the same language. Sometimes the language they speak is similar to the one that their neighbors speak. It could also be very different. A list of tribes of Indian people is located at the end of this book.

American Indians were and continue to be skilled at adapting to the places where they live. From the start, the features of the land where Indian people lived and the plants and animals that they found there influenced their way of life. Their cultures were also shaped by the climate and by neighboring tribes. Tribes that lived in similar regions developed many of the same ways of doing things. For example, they used many of the same medicines and developed similar styles of art. The geographical regions where similar tribes live are called culture areas. The list of tribes at the end of the book is divided into culture areas. Maps of these culture areas are also located at the back of this book. The maps contain the names of tribes that live in these areas.

Over time tribes and their cultures change. Some of the tribes mentioned in this book existed hundreds or thousands of years ago, but they do not exist as groups today. The people themselves did not vanish. Their language changed along with their way of doing things. Sometimes they moved. Sometimes they became part of other tribes.

Other tribal groups, such as the Maya of Mesoamerica, have ancient beginnings and continue to exist today. A glossary of ancient cultures that are mentioned in this book is located on page 113. Here readers will find a short explanation of when these ancient people lived and where they lived. Maps at the end of the book show the location of these ancient peoples as well.

The cultures of the first Americans were so varied and their accomplishments were so many that it would be impossible to write everything about them in one book or even a series of books. The authors apologize in advance for anything in this book that might offend any tribe or band of American Indians. There has been no intention to speak on behalf of any tribe or to pretend knowledge in the ways of all Indian people.

INTRODUCTION

Indian people have lived in the Americas for at least 15,000 years. As they observed the world around them, they developed science. Science is an understanding of the natural processes in the environment. This knowledge enabled American Indians to create technology. Technology is using science to make inventions and to change the environment to meet human needs and wants.

The first Indians of the Americas made spear points from stone for hunting. They also made other tools from stone, bone, and wood. As American Indians gained a working knowledge of sound, they created animal calls and musical instruments. As they developed a working knowledge of light, they made snow goggles that protected their eyes from reflected light, and they learned to polish certain stones to make mirrors. They used chemical processes to make chocolate, dye cloth, and make pottery.

Several groups of Indians mined for metals, including copper, silver, and gold. They invented ways to shape the metal into useful objects as well as jewelry. American Indian engineers created huge earthworks and pyramids. They also made canals and bridges. The Indian people of North America found uses for petroleum, or oil. They shaped the forests by deliberately using fire. The Indians of Meso-america harvested sap from trees and processed it to make rubber.

Indian people throughout the Americas developed number systems that enabled them to count and do math problems. Some used the principles of geometry to build their homes. They carefully observed the planets and stars and learned to predict their movements. The people of Mesoamerica invented the zero, created accurate calendars, and developed writing systems.

The first European explorers and conquistadores in the Americas were impressed by the accomplishments of American Indian people. They adopted some American Indian inventions, such as the chemical process for making chocolate. They ignored many more American Indian inventions. They also ignored much of the scientific knowledge that American Indians possessed. Instead, they focused on taking precious metal and land.

European colonists convinced themselves that because American Indian science and technology were different from European science and technology American Indian knowledge was inferior, or not as good. Today those mistaken beliefs are changing. Every year modern archaeologists (scientists who study the past) make more discoveries about American Indian science and technology. They know that American Indians created technology that was appropriate for the environment in which they lived.

American Indian science and technology is not just a thing of the past. Today a number of American Indians are entering careers as scientists, doctors, and engineers. They carry a rich heritage of curiosity, observation, and invention forward into the future.

Tools and Inventions

Like other peoples of the world, American Indians made tools for hunting, fishing, farming, and preparing food. They created tools for sewing clothing and for making other useful objects, including more tools. The earliest tools that the Indian people of the Americas made were carved from stone and bone. The first people of the Americas probably made tools from wood as well. Because wood decays, these tools did not survive to modern times. The people who lived near the Great Lakes of North America made tools from copper, a metal.

TOOLS

American Indians used flint-knapping to shape and give a sharp edge to their stone tools. To make stone tools, they used special rocks such as flint, obsidian, chert, or quartzite. These stones are fine-grained and hard. When these stones are struck or pressed hard, cone-shaped pieces break off. This creates a razor-sharp edge. American Indians used stone to make spear points, arrows, darts, knives, and scrapers.

Ancient Indians gathered rock that they used for making tools from the surface of the ground. They also mined it from deposits that lay near the Earth's surface. Flint gatherers looked for cracks in these rock deposits. Using rounded river stones as hammers, they drove wooden wedges into the cracks to break off smaller chunks of stone. The chunks of rock that they broke from the deposit are called cores.

Next, early tool makers chipped smaller pieces of rock from the cores with smaller hammer stones. These small pieces are called blanks. Even though they were roughly shaped, the blanks could be used as knives or scrapers. To make spear points, American Indians

Flint knapping produced razor-sharp edges on spear points, knives, and arrows that American Indians flaked from stone. This picture of a Paiute arrow maker and his daughter was taken in northern Arizona territory in about 1880. *(Photograph No. NWDNS-57-PE-1/National Archives and Records Administration—College Park)*

carefully struck the edges of blanks with a small rock or a deer antler to remove small flakes of flint. This is called percussion flaking. Later they learned to use an antler to put pressure on the edge of the blank to remove flakes. This method of flint knapping is called pressure flaking. Pressure flaking gave flint knappers more control over the size of the stone flakes that they removed from blanks.

In 2000 a group of archaeologists claimed to have found the oldest stone spear points in the Americas at Cactus Hill, south of Richmond, Virginia. Tiny pieces of plants and charcoal that they found next to these points are about 15,000 years old. From this evidence, they believe that the stone points are about 15,000 years old as well. Other archaeologists believe that the layers of soil might have been disturbed long ago. The charcoal and the stone points may not have come from the same time period.

Most archaeologists think that the oldest tools in the Americas are Clovis-style points. They are named after Clovis, New Mexico, where they were first found. These points are four to five inches long. American Indian hunters fastened them to wooden shafts, or handles, to make spears for hunting mastodon and wooly mammoth. Clovis points have been found throughout North America, Mesoamerica, and South America. The oldest ones are about 11,500 years old.

Folsom-style points, which American Indians first made about 10,000 to 11,000 years ago, were smaller than Clovis points. They had grooves hollowed out from the surface on both sides. This allowed them to be inserted into the split end of a wooden shaft. Folsom points are named after the Folsom archaeological site in what is now New Mexico.

American Indians continued to use flint knapping to make tools until contact with Europeans. They made arrows that they used for hunting. They also made tools that they used for healing. Aztec doctors used stone scalpels. A scalpel is a tool that is used to make cuts during surgery. The Aztec Empire was established in Mesoamerica in about A.D. 1100. Aztec craftspeople could make metal knives, but stone scalpels were sharper than metal ones.

American Indians also made needles. They used them for sewing pieces of hide (animal skin) together to make clothing. The oldest American Indian sewing needle with an eye was found in Washington State. It was made of bone and is about 10,000 years old.

Another early tool that American Indians made is the wrench. A wrench is a hand tool that is used for twisting. The oldest wrench in Americas was found in Montana. It was made in about 8000 B.C. from bone. This wrench is about 18 inches long and resembles a large, flat needle. The ancient Indians used it to straighten the wooden shafts of their spears.

The arrowheads in this picture were found near Acoma Pueblo in central New Mexico in 1898. In addition to stone points, the picture shows shells that Pueblo Indians traded for with California tribes and bits of pottery. *(Photograph No. NWDNS-79-HPS-6-1553/National Archives and Records Administration—College Park)*

American Indians who lived near the Great Lakes mined copper ore and used it to make metal tools. They began making copper axe blades about 6,000 to 7,000 years ago. They fastened the blades to wooden handles and used them for chopping and as weapons. They made chisels at about the same time. These sharp-edged tools are used to shape wood, stone, or metal. The ancient people of the Great Lakes also made metal drill bits that they attached to wooden handles. These tools are called stick drills. They twisted the stick with their fingers to make holes in wood, bone, and shell.

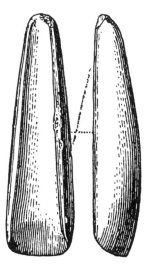

Indian toolmakers made stone gouges to shape wood. American Indians of the Northeast used gouges more often than other tribes. *(U.S. Bureau of Ethnography)*

This old engraving of an American Indian hunter by Currier & Ives was first published in 1845. After contact with Europeans, North American Indians began using metal arrowheads and knives. Artists often drew Indian people in imaginary poses, such as this one of the hunter standing on a bear, in order to portray them as fierce savages. *(Library of Congress, Prints and Photographs Division [LC-USZ62-96250])*

In about 1000 A.D. the Thule people of what is now northern Alaska invented the bow drill for making holes in wood, bone, and ivory. They twisted the string of a bow around the handle of a stick drill. Then they moved the bow back and forth to turn the drill. (The bow was a piece of cord fastened to a longer piece of ivory. The cord caused the ivory stick to bow, or curve.) The Thule made drill bits from the leg bone of a seal. They attached the drill bit to a wooden shaft. They put the shaft into a stone socket with a wooden mouthpiece attached. The mouthpiece allowed the person using the drill to put weight on the shaft while moving the bow back and forth with both hands.

Many groups of North American Indians were using the bow drill at the time Europeans arrived on the continent. They used flexible wood to make their bows. Indians of Mesoamerican and South American also used the bow drill. The Maya people, whose culture arose in about 1500 B.C. in Mesoamerica, used a bow drill with metal bits to make holes in people's teeth. They filled the holes with precious stones. The Maya also used bow drills to drill jade and other stones for jewelry.

American Indians used cord to make saws that were strong enough to cut stone. The Olmec, who lived in Mesoamerica starting in about 1700 B.C., invented the string saw for cutting jade. Jade is a hard green rock. The Olmec put powdered sand or jade on a thin, wet leather strap. They scratched a cut line into the stone and pulled the string saw back and forth over the scratch to cut the jade.

OTHER INVENTIONS

In addition to inventing tools that helped them to work, American Indians invented other items that they used in their daily lives. Some of these inventions were unique to the Americas. Others were invented in other parts of the world as well.

Bow drills such as this one were part of the tool kits used by the Thule people, whose culture arose in what is now Alaska starting in about A.D. 1000. (Photograph No. NRIA-WME-PHOTOS-P898/National Archives and Records Administration—Pacific Alaska Region)

DRILLS FOR MAKING FIRES

Indian people in many parts of the Americas used a drill to start fires. They made it like the bow drill but did not use a drill bit. Turning the wooden stick on soft wood produced friction. Friction is the resistance to motion when two surfaces are slid against each other. The friction made enough heat to light dried grass or small wood shavings.

Trousers

Paleo-Indians in the North American Arctic invented trousers, or pants, as early as 15,000 B.C. Later Inuit men and women of the Arctic and sub-Arctic continued to wear fur trousers. They made them by sewing two leg coverings, or leggings, together in the front and the rear. American Indians of the Northeast and Plains wore moccasins, leggings, and breechcloths that looked like trousers from a distance. (A breechcloth is a strip of leather worn between the legs.) European colonists and fur traders began wearing leather trousers shortly after contact with Indians.

When non-Indians saw Indians smoking pipes at treaty signings, they named the pipes "peace pipes." American Indians of the Great Plains smoked pipes as a way to make allies of other tribes and to make treaties binding. Great Plains Indians used the pipes in religious ceremonies as well. This picture shows John Bear from the Sisseton Dakota Sioux tribe posed with his ceremonial pipe in 1937. *(Photograph No. NRE-75-SIS (PHO)-41, National Archives and Records Administration—College Park)*

Pipes

Moundbuilding Indians, who lived in the southeastern part of what is now the United States, made the first tobacco pipes with bowls and stems. They carved them from stealite, or soapstone, beginning in about 2000 B.C. People of the Hopewell culture lived in the river valleys in the center of North America from about 300 B.C. to A.D. 700. They carved effigy pipes that resembled birds and animals. These figures served as bowls that held the tobacco. They sat on a slender platform that had been drilled to make a stem.

Pipemakers of the Northeast also carved birds and animals on stone pipes. In addition to making stone pipes, the Huron and other tribes also made pipes from clay that they shaped around a grass core. When they hardened these clay pipes in a fire, the grass burned away.

American Indians of the Great Plains carved the bowls of their pipes from pipestone that they quarried from a deposit in the southwestern part of what is now Minnesota. This soft red stone is sometimes called catlinite today. Indian people first began to quarry the stone about 2,300 years ago. They traded it throughout the Great Plains and Midwest.

Often Plains Indians decorated the stems of their pipes with carving, quillwork, and feathers. Many of their pipe bowls were L-shaped or T-shaped, but some were carved to look like birds or animals.

Wheels

For many centuries, scientists who study the past believed that American Indians did not invent the wheel. (In other parts of the world, wheels allowed the animals to pull heavier burdens than they could drag.) Maya potters used a round wooden disk placed on a smooth board to turn their pots when they shaped them. Because the disk did not have an axle, or rod through its center, it was not considered a wheel.

These two wheeled figurines that resemble dogs were found in Veracruz, Mexico. They were made by the Maya. Today they are part of the collection of the National Museum of Anthropology in Mexico City. (David Hixon)

In the 1880s archaeologists found wheeled figures made from clay in El Salvador and Mexico. Maya people had made these wheeled objects between 1200 B.C. and A.D. 900. Later, other archaeologists found wheeled figures at more burial sites in Mexico.

The Maya made the small statues in the shape of animals such as deer, jaguars, monkeys, and dogs. Some of the wheeled statues had moveable parts that could be arranged to form a small platform. The Maya used at least five ways to attach wheels to the axles on these statues. They invented the wheel even though no animals suitable for pulling carts lived in the Americas.

Compasses

A compass uses a lodestone (a magnetic rock that is sometimes called magnetite) to find magnetic north. Magnetic north is the northernmost direction in which the Earth's magnetic field points. It is about 1,400 miles south of the North Pole. The Olmec of Mesoamerica discovered that a lodestone always points toward north and used this knowledge to invent a compass at least 3,000 years ago. The Olmec made a groove in a piece of lodestone. They placed the rock on a large piece of lightweight wood and floated it in water. The groove aligned itself toward magnetic north, like the needle on a

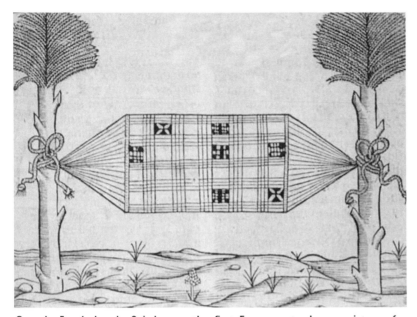

Gonzalo Fernández de Oviedo was the first European to draw a picture of a hammock in 1526. This is a copy of that picture. *(from La Historia General y Natural de las Indias, Hispanic Collection, Library of Congress)*

modern compass does. The Olmec discovered how to make compasses about 1,000 years before the Chinese did. The earliest Chinese compass was made in A.D. 1100. Europeans did not use compasses until A.D. 1178.

Hammocks

Hammocks are large nets or pieces of material that are hung between two trees or poles. American Indians of the Caribbean and Amazon Basin used them for sleeping and sitting. So did people who lived on what is now the Yucatán Peninsula of Mexico.

When explorer Christopher Columbus first arrived in the Caribbean, he was so impressed by hammocks that he wrote about them in his journals. The Spaniards adopted hammocks because they are comfortable, portable, take up little space, and keep sleepers cool. Soon sailors from many European countries slept in hammocks on their ships. Today hammocks are popular as outdoor furniture.

Cradles and Cradleboards

The Inca, who established an empire in what is now Peru in about A.D. 1000, made a baby carrier that was a cradle for newborns and a crib for older babies. It had four legs at the head and two at the foot. The legs at the head were made of two long branches that were bent so that they formed two large Us across the top of the cradle. A blanket placed over them protected the baby's face and head. Mothers tied a long cloth or leather strip around each end of the cradle so that they could carry it on their backs.

Indian people throughout North America made cradleboards for their youngest children. A cradleboard is a stiff frame with a leather pouch attached to it. The pouch holds the baby. The frame can be worn on a person's back or taken off and leaned against a tree or the side of a home. Cradleboards allowed American Indian mothers to keep their babies with them while they worked. They packed dried moss or other substances into the pouch to keep the baby dry and comfortable.

Cradleboards protected babies' heads and shielded their faces from the sun. Some had a narrow shelf on the bottom to keep babies from slipping. Many had a wooden frame that protected the children if the board tipped over. These baby carriers were often decorated with quills as a way of showing how important children were to the family and the tribe.

The Inca of what is now Peru invented a cradleboard with legs. *(After Felipe Guamán Poma de Ayala.* Nueva corónica y buen gobierno)

Appaloosa Horses

Although the Spaniards introduced the horse to North American, by 1710 the Indians of the Northwest had adopted the animal as their own. The Nez Perce of the Plateau liked spotted horses more than others. By carefully breeding horses, they created the breed called the appaloosa today.

These spotted horses are known for their quiet manner and their intelligence. Appaloosas are also known for their endurance and speed. Because they have an easy walk, they are comfortable to ride over long distances. Today ranchers use them when they tend livestock.

Toys

Indians of North America invented tops. They carved them from stone, bone, or wood. To spin a cone-shaped top, a child first wrapped a cord around it and then pulled on the string. The spinning movement of the top was stronger than the pull of gravity. (Gravity is the pull that the

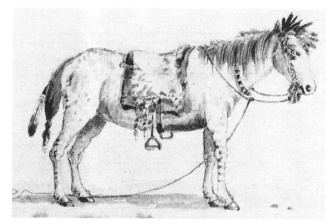

Today the appaloosa horse, first developed by the Nez Perce Indians, has become an officially recognized breed. *(National Archives of Canada, DAP [acc. no. 1981-55-500]. Acquired with the assistance of a grant from the Minister of Communications under the terms of the Cultural Property Export and Import Act.)*

▲▼▲▼▲▼▲▼▲▼▲▼▲▼▲▼▲▼▲▼▲▼▲▼▲▼▲▼▲▼▲

BALLOONS, STILTS, AND KITES

The Olmec were the first people in the world to make rubber balloons. The Maya made stilts that they used for religious ceremonies. (In some North American tribes, stilts were children's toys.) The Maya also made and flew huge kites. These round kites were as large as 15 to 20 feet in diameter. Brightly colored cotton cloth covered their frames. Because the kites were so large, scientists who study the past believe that they were not toys. They may have been used to send signals over long distances.

▼▲▼▲▼▲▼▲▼▲▼▲▼▲▼▲▼▲▼▲▼▲▼▲▼▲▼▲▼▲▼

TIME LINE

These are just some of the tools that American Indians invented.

12,000 B.C. to 8000 B.C.	• Adzes (axelike tools made from stone and wood) • Atlatls (spear throwers that were used for hunting) • Bolas (stones tied to cords that were used for hunting) • Knives made from stone • Manos and metates (stones for grinding seeds) • Needles and pins (made from bone and used for sewing hide clothing) • Spear points • Wrenches
8000 B.C. to 7000 B.C.	• Awls (bone tools for making small holes in leather) • Dippers (made from gourds and used for water and food) • Digging sticks (wooden sticks used to prepare ground for planting) • Spear points with sharp barbs • Baskets • Traps for catching animals
6000 B.C. to 5000 B.C.	• Anvils (stone platforms used when pounding metal) • Fishhooks and awls made from copper • Hammers

Earth exerts on bodies on its surface.) As the top spun, it stood up until friction with the air caused the movement to weaken. Then the top slowed and fell over. The Maya of Mesoamerica also played with tops.

Plains Indians made popguns for their children. They carved a wooden tube with a plunger at one end. A child could place a small stone or other object in the barrel, push the plunger and fire the missile. Archaeologists have found popguns in what is now Peru. Children of the Southwest played with bean shooters. They placed a bean into a tube and blew into it to make the bean fly through the air.

	• Hoes • Knives made from slate • Nets for catching fish • Sinkers made of stone to keep fishing nets from floating
4000 B.C. to 2000 B.C.	• Bows and arrows • Copper tools, including axes, knives, needles, and spear points • Hairpins and combs made from bone • Chisels • Fire-starting kits • Fish traps • Harpoons with detachable heads • Tobacco pipes made from stone
2000 B.C. to 1000 B.C.	• Crowbars (tools used for prying) made from metal • Dip nets for fishing (nets with handles) • Duck decoys • Forceps (medical tools used to grasp or hold) • Pitchforks and rakes • Razors • Scalpels (medical instruments for cutting) • Shovels • Tweezers

2

Sound and Light

American Indians created many inventions that enabled them to use sound and light in their lives. Sound and light are forms of energy that move in waves that have peaks (high points) and valleys (low points) of movement. Sound waves travel through air. Light waves do not depend on the particles in the air in order to travel. They move by disturbing invisible electric and magnetic fields that surround the Earth and are present in space as well. (Other types of electromagnetic waves are radio waves, microwaves, and X-rays.)

Sound and light waves behave in a similar manner. Both of them have amplitude. This is the distance from the peak to the valley. Waves that move up and down only a little have low amplitude. Those that move higher and lower have a higher amplitude. Sound and light waves also have frequency. Frequency is how fast the peaks and valleys of the waves follow one another.

SOUND

Indian hunters throughout the Americas used sound to make animal calls. They designed these calls to make noises similar to those made by the animals that they wanted to hunt. To attract female deer, hunters placed a blade of grass between their thumbs and blew over it to make a sound like that of a fawn, or baby deer. When the hunter blew over the grass, it vibrated. To change the sound, the hunter tightened or loosened the blade of grass. This changed the frequency of the sound waves. (Sound waves that vibrate at a low frequency are low-pitched. Those that vibrate at a high frequency are high-pitched.) Inuit hunters of the Arctic put a pick into the ice and whis-

tled along the shaft to coax a seal or wal-
rus back to a breathing hole it had made in
the ice. The vibration that this made
sounded like the noises that seals make.

American Indian hunters also used
other ways to call animals. They banged
antlers together to imitate the sound of
two stags (male deer) fighting. The
Shoshone people of the Great Basin
banged sticks or rocks together to imitate
the sound of male sheep, or rams, butting
heads.

Music was an important part of lives of
Indian people of the Americas. They
invented a number of percussion and wind
instruments. Percussion instruments, such
as drums and bells, vibrate when they are
struck. Wind instruments, such as flutes
and horns, vibrate when a musician blows
through them.

This Cree man holds an animal call made from birch bark.
American Indians used sound to call caribou and moose that
they were hunting. The shape of this call amplifies the sound
(makes it louder) by making the peaks and valleys of the
sound waves higher and lower than they were to begin
with. *(Edward S. Curtis Collection, Library of Congress, Prints and
Photographs Division [LC-USZ62-123167])*

Drums

Many groups of North American Indians
made drums by stretching hide (animal
skin) over a wooden frame. They controlled the pitch (how high or low the
sound would be) by how tightly they
stretched the hide. The more tightly they stretched the hide, the
higher the drum would sound. Most American Indian musicians
stretched a hide over one end of the wooden frame.

Pueblo people of the Southwest made drums by stretching hide
over both ends of a hollowed log. Indians of the Northwest Coast
placed a wooden plank over a pit in the floor. Then they struck the
plank in order to make it vibrate. They also used drums that they
made from wooden boxes.

The Iroquois people of the Northeast made music with barrel-
shaped drums that they carved from wood. (The Iroquois included the
Oneida, Mohawk, Onondaga, Cayuga, Seneca, and later the Tuscarora
tribes.) Iroquois musicians poured water into their drums before

▲▼▲▼▲▼▲▼▲▼▲▼▲▼▲▼▲▼▲▼▲▼▲▼▲▼▲▼▲▼▲

HOW SOUND WORKS

When the source of the sound vibrates (moves quickly back and forth), the air around it moves back and forth too. The movement passes through the air as sound waves. When these waves reach the ears, they make the eardrum vibrate. The eardrum is a piece of skin that is stretched tightly across a tube in the ear. The vibration of the eardrum makes tiny hairs in the inner ear vibrate as well. The movement of these hairs causes nerve cells to send signals to the brain, which interprets them as sound.

▼▲▼▲▼▲▼▲▼▲▼▲▼▲▼▲▼▲▼▲▼▲▼▲▼▲▼▲▼▲▼

covering the tops with hide. The pitch of these water drums changed depending on how wet the skin top became. The water in the drums gave them an echoing sound that could be heard for long distances. Iroquois musicians also played the tambourine (a small drum that is held in the hand) and a double-headed drum.

Aztec musicians of Mesoamerica used drums that were carved out of wood. Instead of having an open end that was covered with skin, these drums had wooden sound panels carved into them. A type of Aztec drum called the *teponaztli* was shaped like a barrel. It

The Inuit drummers in this picture played for a dance that was held sometime between 1910 and 1930. The Inuit made hand drums with wooden handles attached to their frames. *(Library of Congress Prints and Photographs Division [LC-USZ62-33100])*

▲▼▲▼▲▼▲▼▲▼▲▼▲▼▲▼▲▼▲▼▲▼▲▼▲

MAKING DRUMS SOUND LOUDER
When sound waves bounce back and forth inside the walls of the hollow space inside a drum, they become amplified, or sound louder. Another way to amplify the sound of a drum is to hit the drum harder.

▼▲▼▲▼▲▼▲▼▲▼▲▼▲▼▲▼▲▼▲▼▲▼▲▼

had five tongues that vibrated at different rates when a player struck them with rubber-tipped mallets. Each tongue produced a different sound. The modern marimba is patterned after this Aztec drum.

The Aztec also made drums with hide heads that could be tuned to higher and lower pitches by tightening and loosening them. Some had a single head and others had a double head. Aztec musicians also used small kettle-shaped drums that they beat with their hands.

Musicians of South America also played drums. The Moche, whose culture arose in what is now Peru in about 200 B.C., made tambourines. They also made gongs, large metal disks that are struck with sticks. The Inca made large drums from hollow tree trunks. Another instrument that Inca musicians used was the *chilchil*, a copper disk that they hit with two sticks. This resembled the cymbals that modern musicians play.

Rattles

Indians throughout the Americas made rattles, hollow instruments that contained dried seeds or pebbles. When a musician shook the rattle, seeds or pebbles struck against the container and made it vibrate. North American Indians of the Great Plains made rattles by shaping two pieces of wet rawhide (animal skin that had not been made into leather) over a rock. As the hide dried, it became stiff and took on the shape of the stone. Then the rattle maker put pebbles inside and sewed the two pieces together.

Other American Indians made rattles from turtle shells, gourds, or large cocoons filled with pebbles. They also made rattles from deer hooves. American Indians of the Northwest made rattles from wood, which was plentiful where they lived. Sometimes dancers wore circles of leather with pieces of horn, shells, or hooves attached so that they made music as they moved.

American Indians of Mesoamerica and South America used gourds for rattles instead of hide. Today these instruments are called *maracas*. Maracas are still played in Latin American music.

Bells

The Chavin people, who lived in the northern part of what is now Peru starting in about 1000 B.C., were the first people to make bells in the Americas. The small silver bells that they made looked somewhat like small sleigh bells, known as jingle bells. They used them for jewelry. Later bell makers in South America used copper, gold, and silver to make bells. Toltec metalworkers, who lived in the Valley of Mexico from about A.D. 800 to A.D. 1100, made copper bells that were larger than those that the Moche made. The Toltec traded these bells with the Aztec. The Aztec traded the bells to the Indians of the North American Southwest.

The Aztec musicians in this drawing from the 1500s are playing a number of instruments. The man at the rear is blowing on a conch shell horn. The drummer on the left is playing a drum carved from wood. The panels on the top of the drum vibrate to make sound. *(Library of Congress, Rare Books Division)*

Hunting Bows

Indians of the Plateau Region and the Great Basin played music on the bows that they used for hunting. They made bowstrings from a piece of sinew, the tough fiber that holds an animal's muscle to its bone. They tied this string to each end of a strong and flexible piece of wood so that the wood curved, or bowed. To play music, the bow player held the string of the bow in his teeth and struck it with a stick, changing the shape of his mouth to change the sound. Archaeologists believe that the hunting bow may be the only stringed instrument of the Americas.

Whistles and Horns

American Indians of the Great Plains made whistles from eagle bones. They cut the ends from a long, straight bone and cleaned the marrow from inside the bone so that it would be hollow. Then they cut a notch near one end of the bone tube. This notch was where the whistle's sound was produced. When someone blew into the whistle, the air near the open notch would vibrate. Because the air near the open notch sat on the springy "cushion" of air inside the whistle, it could vibrate very fast, making a high-pitched whistling sound. Whistlers controlled the pitch of their whistles by placing a bit of sticky tree sap into the whistle near the notch. Other North American Indians made whistles from thick, hollow stems of water plants.

The Maya and Aztec made whistles from clay in the shape of animals. They also played horns that were often more than two feet long. They made the horns from clay, wood, or stiff, hollow plant stalks. Mesoamerican musicians also made horns from conch shells.

American Indians who lived in the Andes Mountains of South America also made whistles from clay. These whistles were shaped like small human figures. They were hollow, with holes in the front and in the back. The whistle makers of the Andes put small, empty compartments inside of the whistles that produced tiny echoes, so that the sound of the whistle was different than that of an ordinary whistle. An echo is a sound that continues after its source has stopped.

▲▼▲▼▲▼▲▼▲▼▲▼▲▼▲▼▲▼▲▼▲▼▲▼▲▼▲

A MUSICAL PYRAMID

When people stand at the base of a Maya pyramid and clap their hands, the echoes that they hear sound like the call of the quetzal, a brightly colored bird that was sacred to the Maya. Maya of Mesoamerica built this pyramid, called Kukulkan, in Chichén Itzá in what is now central Mexico about 1,300 years ago. The sound waves produced by clapping hands bounce off hundreds of tall, narrow stone steps. The longer the sound travels, the higher the pitch becomes. No one can be certain, but some archaeologists believe that the Maya designed the steps to imitate the bird call. At least two other Maya pyramids make the same mysterious echo.

The Maya were masters of sound. The ball court that they built at Chichén Itzá is 545 feet long (a little shorter than two football fields laid end to end.). If someone whispers at one end of this Maya ball court, people can hear it at the other end.

▼▲▼▲▼▲▼▲▼▲▼▲▼▲▼▲▼▲▼▲▼▲▼▲▼▲▼

▲▽▲▽▲▽▲▽▲▽▲▽▲▽▲▽▲▽▲▽▲▽▲▽▲

MUSICAL JARS

Moche potters made musical jars in the shape of birds. (The Moche lived on the northern coast of what is now Peru from about 200 B.C. to about A.D. 600.) They designed the jars so that when water was poured out, it forced air through a whistle. They made other jars that were double-walled and had a pellet in the space between the walls. When the jar was moved, the pellet rattled.

▽▲▽▲▽▲▽▲▽▲▽▲▽▲▽▲▽▲▽▲▽▲▽▲▽

The Inca of what is now Peru also made a horn from pottery. It had a hole through the center of the trumpet that doubled back on itself making an S-shape. This allowed the short trumpet to produce deeper tones than one with a straight hole.

Panpipes

The ancient people of what is now Peru were the first to make panpipes, a series of pipes of different lengths fastened together side by side. The different lengths of the pipes produce different pitches. Panpipes are played by blowing air over the ends of the pipes, instead of blowing through them. The ancient Peruvians made the pipes from clay, wood, copper, silver, and gold. The Aztec also made panpipes. American Indians of what is now Florida made copper panpipes. These people of the Southeast traded for copper to make the pipes.

Flutes

Flutes are made from a single hollow tube. They are played by blowing air over one end of the tube. Flutes have finger holes along the side. By covering and uncovering different finger holes, a flute player can make different notes.

In North America, Indians of the Plateau, Northeast, Southeast, and Great Plains cultures made wooden flutes. They played flute music to entertain people. Young men played love songs on the flute

▲▽▲▽▲▽▲▽▲▽▲▽▲▽▲▽▲▽▲▽▲▽▲▽▲▽▲

REED INSTRUMENTS

Some Northwest tribes played reed flutes. They were shaped like tubes and contained one or more reeds. Reeds are flat, thin pieces of wood or plant stalk. They vibrate and make sound when someone blows over them. These reed instruments did not have finger holes.

▽▲▽▲▽▲▽▲▽▲▽▲▽▲▽▲▽▲▽▲▽▲▽▲▽

to impress young women that they wanted to marry. The Sioux Indians (Dakota, Lakota, and Nakota) made cedar flutes with five holes that could play seven notes.

The Aztec of Mesoamerica made flutes of plant stalks, bone, or clay. These flutes had mouthpieces and up to five holes. Inca musicians of South America also made flutes called *quenas*. These flutes could sound up to five notes. The musicians of the Andes Mountains of South America also made music with pottery ocarinas. An ocarina is a flute that is wide in the middle. Musicians of the Andes often made ocarinas in the shape of animals.

LIGHT

In winter American Indians who lived in the area now called the Great Lakes would make a hole in the ice and spear fish through the hole. To do this, they had to be able to see the fish in the water. Light that radiated from the Sun was reflected by the surface of the water. This reflection made it difficult to see beneath the surface of the water. American Indian fishers solved this problem by building a small shelter over the hole that covered their head and shoulders. The shelter blocked most of the sunlight rays from reaching the water so that the fishers could see the fish and spear them.

The Inuit people of the Arctic were faced with a different problem. Because the surface of snow is white and fairly smooth, it reflects a great deal of light. Reflected sunlight glaring from snow can cause snow blindness, a temporary inability to see because of the brightness. The Inuit invented snow goggles to help protect their eyes, so that they could hunt, fish, and travel on sunny winter days. The snow goggles completely covered their eyes and let just enough light in through narrow slits so that the Inuit could see.

American Indians of Mesoamerica used their knowledge of light and reflection to make mirrors. When light strikes the surface of a mirror, it is reflected in the same pattern to produce an image. Mesoamerican Indians made their mirrors so flat, smooth, and shiny that they produced clear and accurate images. The Olmec were the first mirror makers in Mesoamerica. They made mirrors from hematite, a black-to-reddish mineral that is the most common source of iron. The

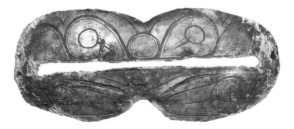

These snow goggles that were made from ivory were found at Point Hope, Alaska. They were probably made between A.D. 100 and A.D. 600. Snow goggles such as these protected the wearer from snow blindness. *(Negative No. 121386/Photo. C. Coles/Courtesy Department of Library Services, American Museum of Natural History)*

This Aztec mirror is made from obsidian, a rock that can be polished so that it reflects light rays. This mirror's frame is made from wood. The image reflected in the mirror is a statue of an Aztec goddess. *(Negative No. 323348, Courtesy Department of Library Services, American Museum of Natural History)*

Maya used iron pyrite for their mirrors. Maya mirrors were the symbol of kings and royalty. Other Mesoamerican culture groups, including the Aztec, used gold, silver, copper, anthracite (hard coal), and obsidian for the mirrors that they made.

Olmec craftspeople shaped magnetite and hematite with stone tools to make mirrors that they used for starting fires using sunlight. They ground the mirrors for these solar fire starters so that they had a concave, or bowed in, surface like a shallow bowl. The concave surface of the fire starter concentrated the rays of sunlight. Their combined energy produced enough heat to set fire to dry grass.

3

Mining for Metals and Metalworking

American Indians who lived near the Great Lakes began to mine copper and shape it into tools and jewelry about 7,000 years ago. Sometimes these ancient people are called the Copper Culture. They are the ancestors of the Anishinabe (Chippewa) people who live near the Great Lakes today. Many archaeologists believe that they were the first people in the world to work with metal. Some Inuit people made iron blades from meteorites, chunks of iron that had fallen from space. Indians of the Circum-Caribbean, Mesoamerica, and North America also gathered metal or mined it and worked it into objects. These metals included gold, silver, copper, and platinum.

American Indians of what are now Michigan's Upper Peninsula, northwest Wisconsin, and northern Minnesota gathered copper nuggets from streams. They also dug hundreds of pits to mine for chunks of copper. The copper that they mined came from veins, or cracks, in bands of lava rock that had been deposited from an ancient volcano millions of years before. Most of this mining took place on what are now Upper Michigan's Keewenaw Peninsula and Isle Royal, an island in Lake Superior.

American Indian copper miners knew the rocks and natural features on the Earth's surface that were clues to where copper was buried. They dug pits only where they were most likely to find the metal. To break chunks of copper from the deposits, they used stones that weighed between half a pound and about 25 pounds. Some of the stones that have been found at old Indian copper mines are grooved so that they could have been fastened to a handle.

American Indians who lived in the northern Great Lakes region dug pit mines for copper. *(Library of Congress Prints and Photographs Division [LC-USZ62-2088])*

American Indians who lived in the Southeast of North America, the Circum-Caribbean, and Mesoamerica panned for gold in streams. The Indians scooped dirt from streambeds into shallow pans with sloping sides. Then they slowly turned the pan or rocked it. The water carried the light particles of earth away. Gold nuggets and flakes, which are heavier than soil, remained in the bottom of the pan. To get deeper layers of soil, the Indian people pushed large, hollow reeds into the bottom of streams. Then they panned the dirt that they collected in the hollow reeds.

The Inca of South America panned for gold as well. They also found another way to way to take gold from streams. Inca engineers built grooved slats from stone and placed them across streams. As water flowed over these stones, sand and gravel were carried downstream. The heavier

American Indians who lived in North America and the Caribbean panned for gold rather than mining it. By the time of the California gold rush, which began in 1849, panning for gold in streams and rivers had become common among non-Indian prospectors. This drawing is from the early 1500s. *(Stock Montage/The Newberry Library)*

This drawing, which was first published in 1591, shows American Indians of the Southeast using hollow reeds to collect gold-bearing sediment from a stream bed. *(Library of Congress, Prints and Photographs Division [LC-USZ62-368])*

gold was trapped by the grooves. When the water level dropped, Inca miners collected gold from the grooves. Much the same method is used in modern placer mining. Inca engineers also changed the direction of streams so that water flowed against cliffs where they had found deposits of gold. The water eroded (washed away) the soil at the base of the cliffs and exposed the gold.

Inca miners also dug shafts and pits for gold and silver ore in mines high in the Andes Mountains. Because this work was so difficult, the Inca had labor laws that protected miners. These laws made sure that they did not endanger their health by working too hard.

METALWORKING IN NORTH AMERICA

The first metalworkers of the northern Great Lakes made tools from copper. These included arrows and spearheads, awls, fishhooks,

SKYWALKERS
Modern American Indian Ironworkers

In 1886 the Dominion Bridge Company of Montreal built the Victoria railroad bridge over the St. Lawrence River at Kahnawake, a community on the Mohawk reserve. In exchange for being able to build the bridge on Mohawk land, the company hired some Mohawk men to work on the bridge. After seeing how fearlessly they walked across the narrow beams that crossed the river, the company trained 12 Indian teenagers to become ironworkers. Their job was to place and connect iron girders, or beams, high above the water.

These first Mohawk workers trained more Mohawk ironworkers. Indian men of other nearby tribes also became ironworkers. These ironworkers helped to build the Empire State Building, the George Washington Bridge, and many other projects in New York City. They

Mohawk ironworkers Bill Sears and Mike Swamp help to build a fire station in Akwesasne, New York, in October 2003. Both belong to Ironworkers Local 440, Utica, New York. *(Ironworkers Local 440)*

knives, axes, and drill bits. In about 3000 B.C. they began making a great deal of jewelry, such as beads and bracelets.

Most of the copper they mined was so pure that it did not need to be processed before shaping it. When the copper was mixed with rock, American Indian miners heated this ore in very hot fires. After it had become white-hot, they put the ore in cold water. As the rock cooled, it cracked and fell apart, making the copper easier to remove. Removing metal from rock by using heat is called smelting.

The Great Lakes metalworkers sometimes hammered copper when it was cold in order to shape it. When they had finished, they

Charlie Edwards, a Mohawk ironworker from Local 440, Utica, New York, works on a New York City high-rise building in 2001. *(Ironworkers Local 440)*

walked the iron girders of bridges and buildings hundreds of feet above the ground. Today American Indian ironworkers work on construction jobs throughout the United States and Canada.

Modern Mohawk ironworkers are called "skywalkers." They helped to build the World Trade Center towers, which were about 1,300 feet tall. The towers were begun in 1966 and finished in 1973. On September 11, 2001, there were about 100 American Indian ironworkers at jobsites in the area. As soon as they heard that planes had smashed into the two towers of the World Trade Center, they rushed to the scene. There they used their knowledge to help rescue hurt people from the buildings. After the towers collapsed, they helped look for survivors in the rubble.

heated it until it was red-hot. Then they slowly allowed it to cool again. This process is called annealing. It makes metal less brittle and less likely to break. Sometimes Indian copper workers heated the copper before they shaped it.

American Indian copper workers traded tools and jewelry with many other groups of Indians. They also exchanged raw copper ore with other Indians, who used it to make tools and jewelry. For the copper, they received shells and obsidian rock. Great Lakes copper nuggets and copper objects have been found in Alberta, Canada; the Mississippi River Valley; and the Northeast. Copper Culture people and their descendants, the Anishinabe, mined and worked copper

▲▽▲▽▲▽▲▽▲▽▲▽▲▽▲▽▲▽▲▽▲▽▲▽▲▽▲

WOMEN'S WORK?

Some archaeologists believe that women were among the first metalworkers in North America. They found a tool kit made up of tools for cooking, sewing, and making copper beads where Copper Culture people stored ore and beads. Among Indian people, cooking and sewing were women's jobs. Perhaps metalworking was a woman's job as well.

▽▲▽▲▽▲▽▲▽▲▽▲▽▲▽▲▽▲▽▲▽▲▽▲▽▲▽

from about 5000 B.C. until the arrival of the French explorers and fur traders in the early 1600s.

The Inuit who lived near Baffin Bay used iron from meteorites to make knives. Baffin Bay separates Greenland from Canada. Inuit people told European explorers that the metal had come from "iron mountains" that had been thrown from the sky. In 1894 explorer Richard Peary found three large chunks of iron meteorite that the Inuit people called "Woman," "Dog," and "Tent." The explorer and his crew removed the 1,000-pound dog, the 6,000-pound woman, and the 100-ton tent to New York.

This old drawing shows an Aztec metalworker heating copper in a fire. Mesoamericans learned some of their metalworking techniques from the metalworkers of South America. *(Library of Congress, Rare Books Division)*

METALWORKING IN SOUTH AMERICA

American Indians of what are now Bolivia and Ecuador began working with gold and copper in about 1900 B.C. Later they worked with silver, platinum, and other metals. By about 1400 B.C. metalworkers of the Andes Mountains began making metal foil by hammering gold into thin sheets. Early South American metalworkers used nearly pure metal ores.

The Chavin people, who lived in what is now Peru from 1000 B.C. to 200 B.C., discovered how to weld. Welding is joining pieces of metal together with heat. Chavin metalworkers welded hammered sheets of silver and gold to make three-dimensional objects. They also discovered how to solder sheets of gold together by placing another metal that had been treated with acid along the joint and heating it until it melted. In addition, they stapled sheets of metal together by pushing wires through small holes in the sheets and then bending the wires.

The Moche, who lived in what is now Peru starting in about 200 B.C., learned how to smelt ore in order to remove metal from rock. A Moche metalworker would build a fire in a baked clay pot that was about three feet across. Then the metalworker blew into a copper tube that was about five feet long. The oxygen made the fire burn hotter. The Moche also used a wind furnace to smelt ore. Metal workers set the furnace so that the wind blew into the hole in the back. Then they built a fire with charcoal in a hole at the front of the furnace. The wind made the fire hot enough to smelt ore. The Moche also knew how to anneal metal.

By about 200 B.C. the Moche had discovered how to shape copper by casting it, or pouring it into molds. At first they did sand casting. To make a sand casting, the metalworker made a model of the object that he or she wanted to cast. When it was finished, the worker pushed it into wet sand to make an impression. After the model was removed, the metalworker poured melted metal into the sand. When the cast had cooled and hardened, the metalworker removed it from the sand. The Moche used sand casting to make weapons and farming tools.

Moche metalworkers also invented lost wax casting. First they created a wax model of what they wanted to make. Then they covered the wax with a thick coating of clay, leaving a small opening. After the clay had dried, the workers heated it, so that the wax melted and flowed through the opening. Then they poured melted metal into the clay form and let it cool. Finally they broke the clay form and removed the object.

The Moche also invented alloys, or mixtures of metals. By adding copper to gold, metalworkers lowered the melting point of gold.

MERCURY

Mercury is a metal that is silvery in color. It is very poisonous and is liquid at room temperature. It is obtained from cinnabar, a red-colored rock that contains both mercury and sulfur. The Inca mined cinnabar in the Andes Mountains. The Maya of Mesoamerica also knew how to remove mercury from cinnabar. Cinnabar was an important trade item in northern South America and in Mesoamerica.

PLATINUM

Platinum is a very hard metal that has a melting point of about 1,770°C (3,218°F). American Indian metalworkers in what is now Ecuador made granules (tiny pieces) of platinum and silver. Then they mixed them together and heated them. The silver lowered the melting point of the platinum. The metalworkers could hammer the softer platinum and silver alloy into the shape they desired. Europeans were unable to work platinum into objects before the 1800s.

This alloy, which was called *tumbaga,* was easier to shape than gold. Objects made from tumbaga had some copper on the surface. Moche metalworkers dipped an object in acid that removed the copper. This left a thin film of gold on the surface so that the object looked as if it had been made from pure gold. The Moche also made bronze from tin and copper.

Moche metalworkers invented other ways to gold-plate the things that they made. Sometimes they hammered thin gold foil onto a copper object. Then they heated it until the gold melted. Sometimes they poured melted gold over the object to coat the surface. They also discovered how to deposit a thin coat of gold using electricity that arises in a chemical solution. This is called electroplating.

Later the Inca continued the metalworking tradition in South America. They made beautiful gold jewelry and small statues of gold and silver. Inca builders used gold in their temple buildings. They made a huge gold disk that reflected the sun's rays for the Temple of the Sun in Cuzco, their capital. The Temple of the Sun was also covered with

The Aztec metalworker shown in this drawing is casting an object from gold. The melted gold flows from the furnace to a clay-covered mold. When the gold hardens, the metalworker breaks the mold to remove the object.
(Library of Congress, Rare Books Division)

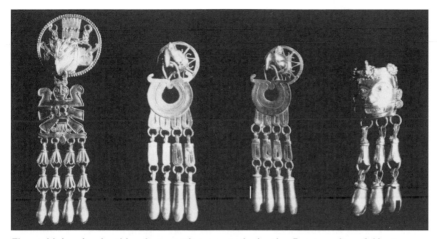

The gold jewelry in this photograph was made in the Zapotec city of Monte Albán. The Zapotec were skilled metalworkers. By 200 B.C. about 10,000 people lived in Monte Albán, and the city grew to 25,000 residents. Although Monte Albán was later abandoned, Zapotec culture remained. *(Library of Congress, Prints and Photographs Division [LC-USZ62-112915])*

sheets of gold. The Inca filled the courtyards of their temples with golden statues of llamas and corn plants. One temple had an entire garden of plant statues that were made from silver and gold.

METALWORKING IN MESOAMERICA

Many archaeologists believe that between A.D. 500 and A.D. 1,000 South American metalworkers traveled with traders to the west coast of what is now Mexico. At about this time, Mesoamerican Indians suddenly began working with alloys of silver, copper, arsenic, and gold. They also began making lost wax castings. Their knowledge of how to work with metal then spread throughout Mesoamerica.

The Mixtec, whose culture flourished from A.D. 800 to A.D. 1500, used lost wax casting to make golden jewelry, masks, breastplates, and dishes. They decorated these with filigree. Filigree is fine wires that are soldered to another piece of metal. The Mixtec also created designs by hammering on the back of a piece to produce raised designs on the front. The Toltec, who lived in Mesoamerica from about A.D. 950 to 1200, became famous for their metalwork, as well. The Zapotec of southern Mexico also became skilled metalworkers.

At first the Aztec relied on Zapotec, Toltec and Mixtec metal-workers to make their jewelry and other items from metal. Eventually they learned how to work with metal themselves. Aztec

Spanish conquistadores used llamas to carry Inca silver and gold to their ships in order to send it to Spain. The Spaniards destroyed jewelry and sculptures by melting them down into bars of precious metal. *(Library of Congress, Prints and Photographs Division [LC-USZ62-68525])*

metalworkers used lost wax casting to make luxury items such as jewelry and bells. Aztec gold workers had their own guilds. These organizations set quality standards for the objects that they made. The workers lived in their own neighborhood in the Aztec capital of Tenochtitlán.

THE SPANIARDS' QUEST FOR GOLD AND SILVER

Christopher Columbus brought back only a small amount of gold from his voyages in the late 1400s, but that was enough to start a gold rush. The Spaniards soon sent expeditions to find more gold. Hernán Cortés conquered the Aztec and sent his men throughout what had been their empire to search for gold. Francisco Pizarro, who conquered the Inca, also sought the source of their gold. A group of conquistadores led by Hernando de Soto traveled to what is now Florida and the Carolinas. Francisco Vásquez de Coronado led conquistadores to what is now New Mexico and Arizona.

When the early conquistadores saw the beautiful gold and silver jewelry worn by Aztec and Inca rulers and the golden statues in their temples, they were amazed. By European standards, the Aztec and Inca were wealthy beyond imagination. The Spaniards' shock quickly turned to greed. They melted the gold and silver

Spanish conquistadores forced American Indians to mine silver and gold for them in Mesoamerica and South America. Here an Indian is shown working a bellows imported by the Spaniards. When the Spaniards discovered that bellows could not make fires hot enough to melt metal in the mountains, they used methods of the Inca, including the wind furnace. *(Library of Congress, Prints and Photographs Division [LC-USZ62-1492])*

work and formed it into bars. Then they shipped the bars back to Europe. They kept some of the gold and silver for themselves.

Whenever the Spaniards found gold deposits in the Earth, they enslaved American Indians and set them to mine it. By 1542, the amount of gold shipped to Europe from the Americas tripled the amount of wealth Europeans had. By 1600, the amount of gold and silver in Europe had increased by eight times.

NAVAJO SILVERSMITHING

Today the Navajo (Dineh) people are known for working with silver. Atsidi Sani is the first Navajo (Dineh) silversmith. In 1853 he began making silver jewelry. He taught his sons how to work with silver too. Soon the craft spread. Navajo silversmiths began by making

The Navajo began making silver and turquoise jewelry in the mid-1800s. This 1870 photo of a Navajo silversmith shows the early stages of a style of jewelry that would later include turquoise stones and become popular throughout the world. *(Photograph No. NWDNS-75-BAE-2421-b-6/Bureau of Indian Affairs/National Archives and Records Administration—College Park)*

bells from quarters and creating small tobacco cases. The Navajo learned how to cast silver from Mexican metalworkers who made castings in clay. It is very likely that some of their teachers were descendants of Toltec, Aztec, or Zapotec metalworkers.

Atsidi Chom was the first Navajo silversmith to set turquoise into silver. He made his first silver and turquoise ring in the late 1870s. Soon the Zuni and Hopi began making silver and turquoise jewelry too. Today the work of Navajo, Zuni, and Hopi jewelry makers is known throughout the world.

TIME LINE	
5000 B.C.	Indians of the Northern Great Lakes mine copper and discover how to anneal metal.
1900 B.C.	South American Indians begin working with gold.
1000 B.C.	Miners and metalworkers of the upper Great Lakes have by now developed a complex trade network based on copper.
200 B.C.	Moche metalworkers of what is now Peru learn to cast metal in order to shape it.
A.D. 500 to A.D. 1000	South American knowledge of metalwork techniques travels to Mesoamerica.
A.D. 1853	Atsidi Sani invents a style of southwestern silver jewelry that is still popular today.
A.D. 1870s	Atsidi Chom adds turquoise to the Navajo jewelry.

4

Petroleum and Rubber

American Indians who lived in areas where petroleum seeped to the surface of the Earth used it as fuel and as a skin lotion. Petroleum, or oil, is a naturally occurring liquid that contains hydrogen and carbon. Indian people gathered natural deposits of thick petroleum, called asphalt, and used that to waterproof baskets and clothing. American Indians who lived in the Yucatán Peninsula of Mesoamerica and the Amazon Basin of South America collected latex from rubber trees. They used the latex to waterproof clothing. They also invented a way to process the latex in order to make rubber balls as well as other items. American Indians traded petroleum and rubber, and they traded the goods that they made from these materials.

PETROLEUM

Petroleum comes from single-celled plants and animals that lived in oceans that covered many parts of the Earth millions of years ago. When the plants and animals died, they sank to the bottom of these ancient seas and began to decay.

The decaying plants and animals were covered with sediment (mud and sand that sank to the bottom of water). Over millions of years, more sediment was deposited on top of the plants and animals. This created pressure on the plants and animals and caused the temperature to rise. The rising pressure and temperature caused sediments to harden into rocks. It also turned the plants and animals into hydrocarbons. The hydrocarbons formed crude oil and natural gas that collected in pockets in the sedimentary rock beneath the surface

Pennsylvania businessman Edwin L. Drake believed he could make money by selling oil as fuel for lamps. He did not discover oil. He drilled for oil at a site where American Indians had been gathering it for more than 400 years. *(Library of Congress, Prints and Photographs Division [LC-USZ62-87910])*

of the Earth. When the rock cracked or buckled, oil and gas seeped to the Earth's surface.

North American Indians dug pits in many parts of what is now Pennsylvania in order to collect oil. They began this digging in about A.D. 1415. The pits that they dug along what is now called Oil Creek were from 15 to 20 feet deep. The Indians made walls around the

At first Drake dug a deep pit as the Indians before him had done, but the walls caved in. The next year he drilled a well that caved in as well. His idea of pounding a pipe into the ground to keep the hole from collapsing was successful in 1859. Drake called his oil company the Seneca Oil Company. *(Library of Congress, Prints and Photographs Division [LC-USZ62-87910])*

inside of the collection pits with wood that they cut with stone axes. This wood kept the earthen walls of the pits from caving in. Archaeologists have found ladders near the pits. The Indians made them by carving notches into pine tree logs. They also made scoops from twigs and branches to col-

△▽△▽△▽△▽△▽△▽△▽△▽△▽△▽△▽△▽△▽△▽△▽△

OIL AS MEDICINE

Europeans believed that oil was medicine. In 1539 the Spanish conquistadores sent oil from what is now Venezuela to the Holy Roman Emperor, Charles V. They gave it to him to treat his gout, a painful disease of the joints. Later, North American druggists sold what they called "Seneca oil" to treat cuts and rheumatism, another joint disease.

▽△▽△▽△▽△▽△▽△▽△▽△▽△▽△▽△▽△▽△▽△▽△▽

lect oil. Scientists believe that the Indians filtered the oil through leaves and clay. In addition to collecting oil in pits, American Indians skimmed it off the surface of the creek with feathers.

The French general Louis Montcalm was the first European to mention American Indians and oil. He watched Seneca Indians performing a ceremony next to Oil Creek and saw that they had set fire to the oil that seeped from the ground. Both the Seneca and other Iroquois used oil to fuel ceremonial fires. They also used it as a skin lotion, much like today's petroleum jelly.

Asphalt is the dark, thick substance that remains when lighter hydrocarbons in petroleum evaporate into the air. The Chumash, a California tribe, collected asphalt from tar pits near what is now Los Angeles. People of the Yokuts, Maidu, and Achomawi tribes also gathered and used asphalt. The Chumash, who lived nearest the oil seeps, traded asphalt with other Indians. In exchange, they obtained soapstone, salt, hides, fur, and food.

The Chumash used asphalt to caulk their canoes in order to keep water from leaking inside of them. To do this, they crumbled dry asphalt and heated it in a stone bowl. They mixed the asphalt with pitch (hardened tree sap). Then they added red ocher, a fine soil, to thicken it. Chumash boatbuilders poured the mixture onto the surface of their canoes with ladles that they had carved from soapstone. They spread the caulking with willow bark brushes and scraped the excess off with bone scrapers. When the caulking started to leak, the boatbuilders used a hot stone to melt the asphalt and cover the hole.

The Chumash people and their neighbors also used asphalt to seal long-necked baskets that they used as water containers. They coated the insides of the baskets by filling them with pebbles that they had

> Indian people who lived on the coast of what is now California made dishes by using asphalt to plug the holes in abalone shells.

California-area Indians used asphalt to coat the insides of some of their baskets in order to waterproof them. These baskets were made by the Pomo, who are thought to be the most skilled basketmakers in North America. *(Edward S. Curtis Collection, Library of Congress, [LC-USZ62-87910])*

dipped into hot asphalt. Then they shook the baskets so the asphalt-covered stones would brush against the inside walls. Basket weavers sometimes used asphalt to coat the outsides of their baskets as well.

California Indians used asphalt as a glue. This glue held spear points and arrow points to wooden shafts. Indians glued plant fibers to sticks to make brushes. They also glued small pieces of shell on objects that they made from stone, bone, or wood to decorate them. Yokuts hunters made special arrows that they used for hunting birds that lived in the water. They made doughnut-shaped rings out of reeds and slid them onto the shafts of their arrows. These rings, which they glued in place with asphalt, made the arrows skim along the water's surface.

RUBBER

Rubber is made from latex, a sticky sap that is produced by rubber trees that grow to be from 30 to 60 feet tall. These trees grow in parts of Mesoamerica and in South America along the Amazon River. The Olmec of Mesoamerica were the first people to process latex to make rubber. The Olmec traded rubber and the things that they made from it with other groups of Indian people. The word *Olmec* means "the Rubber People."

Although the Olmec are best known for making and trading rubber, other people who lived where rubber trees grew were also skilled at processing rubber. The Maya made rubber to waterproof clothing. The Quecha of northern part of what are now Peru and Bolivia called the rubber tree *caoutchouc*. Their culture flourished at the time of the Inca, about A.D. 1000. The Quecha made rubber to coat ropes and baskets that they used for holding water.

Indian people had a routine for harvesting latex from rubber trees. Often they worked in teams. Two people would open a trail through the jungle. This trail connected about 100 rubber trees. To

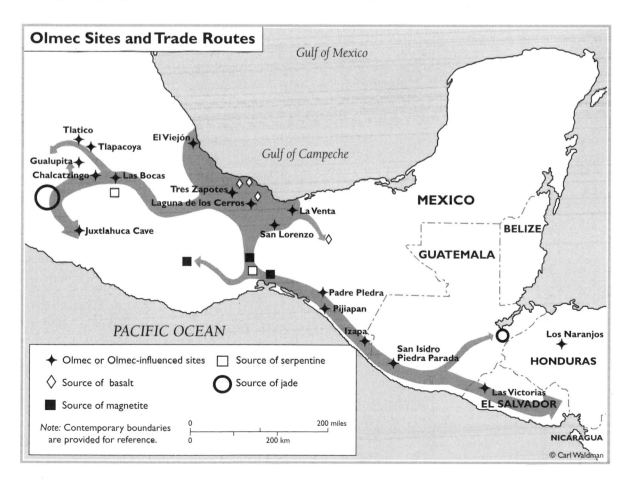

Olmec Sites and Trade Routes

This picture of a rubber-tree trunk with a modern collection cup shows how the tree's bark has been cut so that latex will flow into the cup. Rubber latex is still harvested today in much the same way as the Olmec and Maya harvested it hundreds of years ago. *(Library of Congress, Prints and Photographs Division [LC-USZ62-95012])*

remove the sap from a tree, the rubber collectors made a slash in the bark with a small stone hatchet. If the tree was a large one, they would make several slashes. These slanting cuts allowed latex to flow from the cambium, or inner bark, of the tree. The cambium of a tree is a thin layer of cells that keeps the tree alive and controls its growth. Rubber harvesters were careful not to damage rubber trees when they cut through the outer bark.

After the harvesters slit the bark, they attached a clay cup to the tree at the bottom of the slits. The latex seeped from the cuts and pooled in the cup. As the collectors moved back along the pathway, they emptied the cups that were filled with latex into gourd buckets. They stopped at each tree to remove small slivers of bark from the cut in order to keep the latex flowing. One day's work would amount to only about one or two gallons of latex.

In its natural state latex from rubber trees is not very useful. Even after it has been cooked and thickened, it becomes so soft in hot weather that it loses its shape. Raw latex and hardens and cracks in cold weather. The Maya, Olmec, and Quecha found a way to solve this problem by curing, or treating, it. The process of curing rubber is called vulcanization today.

HOW VULCANIZATION WORKS

Latex from plants is made up of polymers, long chains of identical molecules. A molecule is the simplest part of a chemical compound or element. The chemicals that are added to latex when it is cured form links between the polymers in the latex. In addition to making rubber that keeps its shape in hot and cold weather, vulcanization also makes rubber elastic. When it is stretched and released, it comes back to its original shape.

When the Indians had brought the latex to their rubber-making camp, they picked out bits of leaves and twigs that had fallen into it. Next they built a fire of palm nuts. The smoke from these nuts contained phenols, acids that are made up of hydrogen and oxygen like hydrogen peroxide is. Then the Indians built a funnel-shaped

This rubber worker from Brazil is holding latex over a fire to smoke it in the manner that American Indians first used. When American Indians used latex to make hard rubber balls, they held it in the smoke longer than when they used it to waterproof cloth. The more chemicals that are added to latex, the harder it becomes. *(Library of Congress, Prints and Photographs Division [LC-USZ62-95012])*

▲▼▲▼▲▼▲▼▲▼▲▼▲▼▲▼▲▼▲▼▲▼▲▼▲▼▲

SYRINGES

Ancient rubber workers covered clay forms with latex to make syringes. Syringes are hollow bulbs that are shaped with a rubber tube on one end. Today in Mexico, latex gatherers are called *seringuerio*. This means "maker of syringes."

▼▲▼▲▼▲▼▲▼▲▼▲▼▲▼▲▼▲▼▲▼▲▼▲▼▲▼

chimney over the fire to concentrate the smoke. When the smoke contacted the latex, it caused a chemical reaction.

Ancient rubber workers of South America and Mesoamerica made water bottles by holding a clay form that they had shaped like a bottle over the smoke from the fire. Then they carefully poured latex over it until between 20 and 25 thin coats had been applied. After they let the bottles dry for about five days, they washed

A South American Indian carries an explorer down the Amazon River on his boat. After non-Indians discovered how to treat rubber in order to make it useful in 1844, the demand for latex rose sharply. *(Library of Congress, Prints and Photographs Division [LC-USZ62-109130])*

the clay from the forms and stuffed the bottle with dried grass to harden for several months. After the bottles were hard, they were ready to fill with liquid. The American Indian rubber workers made shoes, hollow rubber balls, and soles for sandals in the same way.

According to some reports, they often used their own feet as molds to make rubber shoes. Rubber workers also coated cloth with cured rubber to make waterproof clothing, including capes and head coverings. Waterproof clothing was important in the rain forest, which sometimes receives up to nine feet of rain each year.

In addition to using smoke to cure rubber, American Indians also mixed latex with the juice from morning glory vines, which are high in sulfur. (Sulfur is the main chemical used in modern rubber processing throughout the world.) They used this process to make solid rubber balls and bricks of rubber that they used for trading.

The Olmec and Maya traded rubber balls to other Mesoamerican people and taught them how to play a ball game. This ancient version of basketball used stone hoops instead of baskets. Stone ball

This hollow clay whistle in the shape of a Maya ballplayer shows him holding a rubber ball. Rubber balls that American Indians made have been found throughout Mesoamerica. The earliest ones were made in about 1000 B.C. *(Photograph Courtesy of the Milwaukee Museum)*

▲▽▲▽▲▽▲▽▲▽▲▽▲▽▲▽▲▽▲▽▲▽▲▽▲▽▲▽

WHY DO RUBBER BALLS BOUNCE?

If a person drops a rubber ball, gravity pulls it to the floor. When it hits the floor, it changes shape. Some of the polymer chains (strings of identical molecules) in the rubber ball become packed tightly together. Others are pulled apart. When the polymer chains in a rubber ball snap back into their original places, the ball regains its shape. The kinetic energy (movement energy) stored in the ball causes it to move through the air on the rebound. Any energy that is left over turns into heat. The harder a person throws a ball, the more energy he or she puts into it, and the higher the ball bounces.

▽▲▽▲▽▲▽▲▽▲▽▲▽▲▽▲▽▲▽▲▽▲▽▲▽▲▽▲▽

After the demand for rubber increased, boats such as this one took workers who harvested latex to huge rubber plantations owned by non-Indians. *(Library of Congress, Prints and Photographs Division [LC-USZ62-83664])*

courts designed for playing this game have been found throughout Mesoamerica and in the Southwest of North America.

Christopher Columbus first encountered rubber on his second voyage to what is now Haiti from 1493 to 1496. He saw balls "made of the gum of a tree." Later Spanish explorers brought reports of the rubber and ball games back to Europe. Explorers imported small amounts of rubber to Europe, but Europeans did not know how to cure it so that it was useful. They used latex to make erasers, which the English called rubbers. By the early 1800s Europeans were making small quantities of rubber syringes and galoshes.

Non-Indians paid no attention to how American Indians had treated rubber, so for years they did not believe that rubber was useful. Finally, American inventor Charles Goodyear accidentally dropped latex mixed with sulfur on a hot stove. He had reinvented the process that the American Indians of the Amazon Basin and Mesoamerica had known for centuries. Goodyear patented his discovery in 1844.

Rubber has become an important part of modern life. Most of today's rubber comes from commercial plantations in Thailand, Indonesia, Malaysia, and Sri Lanka, rather than the Amazon Basin, where it originated. In the Amazon Basin of South America, some Indian people still make rubber by hand as their ancestors did.

TIME LINE	
8000 B.C.	Some groups of American Indians living east of the Missouri River gather asphalt from natural oil seeps to waterproof baskets.
1600 B.C.	The oldest known rubber objects are being made by Mesoamerican Indians, who probably were working with rubber earlier than this.
A.D. 1415	Tribes of the Northeast begin collecting oil from oil seeps in what is now Pennsylvania.
A.D. 1493	Explorer Christopher Columbus becomes the first European to see a rubber ball on what is now the island of Hispaniola (modern Haiti and the Dominican Republic.

5 Chemistry

 Chemistry looks at how the elements that make up matter behave. Matter is anything that takes up space or has weight. An element is one of more than 100 substances that make up all matter in the world. American Indians had a working understanding of chemistry. They invented chemical processes to make foods that contain toxic (poisonous) substances safe to eat. The Indian people of Mesoamerica discovered ways to turn bitter cacao beans into chocolate. They also found a method to transform vanilla beans into vanilla, a flavoring that tastes nothing like the beans in their original state.

Indians throughout the Americas found ways to fire, or bake, clay and turn it into pottery. They used acid to etch designs into shells. They dyed cloth that has retained its color for thousands of years. American Indian metalworkers of South America discovered how to electroplate metal objects. Electroplating uses chemicals to generate a current that deposits a thin coating of one metal on top of another metal.

MAKING FOOD SAFE TO EAT

American Indians of the Northeast, Southeast, and California culture areas ate shelled acorns that they ground into meal. Acorns, the nuts from oak trees, contain high levels of tannins. Tannins are naturally occurring chemicals that taste bitter. Large amounts of tannins reduce the amount of protein that the body can absorb and can even be poisonous. American Indians discovered a way to process acorns in order to remove the tannins from them. Indians who lived in what is now California began processing and eating acorns between 11,000 and 12,000 years ago.

This Pomo woman is cooking acorns that she has first prepared by washing out the tannins that raw acorns contain. This picture was taken in 1924. Before contact with Europeans, American Indians did not have iron pots. They boiled their food by dropping hot rocks into stone, wood, or pottery containers that were filled with water and the food that they were cooking. *(Edward S. Curtis Collection, Library of Congress Prints and Photographs Division [LC-USZ62-103072])*

They figured out that tannins dissolve in water. American Indians of the Northeast and Southeast placed baskets of ground acorn meal in streams. They allowed the water to run through the basket that contained the meal for at least a day. This washed away most of the tannins. California Indians placed acorn meal in a hole that they had scooped from the sand along a stream bank. Then they poured water over the meal many times so that the tannins would seep into the ground with the water. The Pomo Indians of California mixed a small amount of fine clay with acorn meal before they baked it into flat bread. Modern scientists have found that the clay neutralized, or canceled the effects, of the tannins.

▲▽▲▽▲▽▲▽▲▽▲▽▲▽▲▽▲▽▲▽▲▽▲▽▲▽▲

STRONG MEDICINE

Many American Indian medicines contained chemicals called alkaloids. The alkaloids were what affected the human body. American Indian healers had a great deal of knowledge about the effects of plants on people. They were careful not to give their patients too much of a plant medicine. Too much medicine could make people sicker or even cause them to die. Too little medicine would not have any effect.

▽▲▽▲▽▲▽▲▽▲▽▲▽▲▽▲▽▲▽▲▽▲▽▲▽▲▽

Other American Indians also mixed small amounts of clay with their food in order to make some foods taste better and to make other foods that contained toxins, or poisons, safe to eat. Indians of the Southwest ate white clay with wild potatoes that contained alkaloids. An alkaloid is a compound that contains nitrogen. In large amounts alkaloids are poisonous to humans. The clay absorbed the alkaloids so that they were not released into the bloodstream of people who ate the wild potatoes. American Indians of the Andes Mountains of South America also ate a kind of clay called kaolin with wild potatoes to neutralize the toxins that the potatoes contained.

Manioc is a plant with a starchy root. It has been grown and harvested for thousands of years by Indian people in what are now Mexico, Guatemala, northern Brazil, and the Caribbean. Some types of manioc plants contain a poison called prussic acid, or hydrocyanic acid, in small sacs under the covering of the root. When people eat the roots from these manioc plants, the acid in their stomachs turns the hydrocyanic acid into cyanide, a deadly poison.

American Indians knew that the toxin in manioc is contained in the juice of the root. They peeled raw manioc roots and then shredded them on graters made of stone chips that they had set into wooden boards. Next they squeezed the juice out of the grated manioc roots with presses. Sometimes they put the shredded roots in nets so that the juice would drip from them. After the juice had drained from the manioc they roasted it, ground it into meal, and made it into flat bread.

The Indians of the Amazon and Caribbean discovered that they could make the juice from manioc roots safe to eat if they heated it. In addition to hydrocyanic acid, manioc juice contains a chemical called linase. When they heated the juice to the right temperature, the linase neutralized the hydrocyanic acid so that it was no longer a poison. They used the heated manioc juice to tenderize tough pieces of meat and for making soup. Today heated manioc juice continues to be used as a meat tenderizer in many parts of the world.

MAKING CHOCOLATE AND VANILLA

The Maya discovered how to make chocolate from the cacao trees that they planted and harvested in about A.D. 200. Cacao harvesters picked the pods from the trees. Then they split them open and scooped out the 20 to 50 cream- to lavender-colored seeds that were inside of each pod. They let the seeds dry.

Next they fermented the seeds. When a substance is fermented, the molecules that make it up break apart into simpler substances. (Molecules are groups of atoms, which are the smallest pieces of elements.) The sugar in the cacao seeds turned into lactic and acetic acid. This caused the cacao seeds to taste less bitter. A chocolate flavor began to develop. Fermenting the seeds also turned them brown. Next the chocolate makers roasted the beans and they removed the thin shell that covered each bean. Finally they ground them to make a paste. It took about 400 beans to make a pound of chocolate.

In 1519 the Aztec emperor Montezuma served the Spanish conquistador Hernán Cortés and his men chocolate drinks. Cortés took cacao beans and chocolate powder to Spain. At first Europeans believed that chocolate was a drug, but by 1580 it was a popular

These cacao harvesters from Ecuador, whose pictures were taken in 1907, are removing the pods from cacao trees, much as the Maya did hundreds of years before. Cacao is the basis for chocolate. *(Library of Congress Prints and Photographs Division [LC-USZ62-98874])*

▲▽▲▽▲▽▲▽▲▽▲▽▲▽▲▽▲▽▲▽▲▽▲▽▲▽▲▽▲▽▲

THE FIRST CHOCOLATE DRINKS

The Maya used chocolate paste to make hot and cold drinks. The Aztec also drank chocolate drinks. Both the Maya and Aztec sweetened the drinks with honey. The Aztec believed that chocolate was a medicine as well as a food.

▼▲▼▲▼▲▼▲▼▲▼▲▼▲▼▲▼▲▼▲▼▲▼▲▼▲▼▲▼▲▼

drink for Spanish nobility. Today chocolate has become popular throughout the world. Every day nine out of 10 Americans eat some form of chocolate.

Indian people of Mesoamerica made vanilla from the bean, or seed, of a special type of orchid. American Indian farmers who lived near what is now Veracruz, Mexico, planted and harvested these orchids for their seedpods. They let the vanilla pods wilt. Wilting produced enzymes. Enzymes are proteins that spark chemical reactions. Then they heated the beans to speed the chemical reaction and to prevent them from rotting. Heating also turned the pods a dark brown color. Next the Indian vanilla makers dried the pods. Finally they put them in closed boxes and kept them there for about three months so that the flavor would deepen. The chemical process that the American Indians invented released an oil in the pods and beans that is called vanillin. This oil gives vanilla its flavor.

The Spaniards took vanilla beans to Europe, but Europeans did not make their own vanilla until the late 1700s. Before that they did not understand the steps that were necessary to make the pods taste and smell like vanilla. The American Indian vanilla makers of Veracruz kept their method a secret from the Spaniards for more than 100 years. Today the Totonac Indian people from the state of Veracruz in Mexico continue to grow orchids for vanilla.

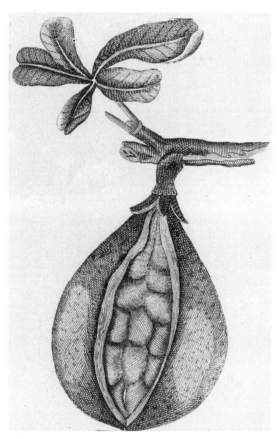

François Froger, a Frenchman who traveled to the Caribbean and Brazil in the late 1600s drew this picture of what he called a Mapou pear. (Mapou is a village in Haiti.) Although cacao leaves look different than these, the pod appears to be a cacao pod. After the French took Haiti from the Spaniards in 1684, they planted many cacao plantations in that country. The Spaniards had taken Haiti from the American Indians who lived there. *(Library of Congress, Prints and Photographs Division [LC-USZ62-71973])*

MAKING POTTERY

Indians throughout the Americas made pottery. The oldest pottery in the Americas was found in the Amazon Basin. It was made between 7,000 and 8,000 years ago. American Indians made their pottery from clay that they shaped into pots, jars, and dishes and then heated in a fire. For the most part, women were the potters.

Clay is finely grained soil. It can be shaped when it is wet. As it dries the clay becomes stiffer. When it is completely dry, it is very fragile and

American Indians caused a chemical reaction in clay when they heated it. This reaction made the clay harden into pottery. This photo of potters at Santa Clara Pueblo in New Mexico was taken in 1916.
(Photograph No. NWDNS-75-N-PU-40/National Archives and Records Administration at College Park)

▲▽▲▽▲▽▲▽▲▽▲▽▲▽▲▽▲▽▲▽▲▽▲▽▲▽▲

A PERMANENT REACTION

The chemical reaction that takes place when pottery is heated to a high enough temperature does not reverse itself. Pieces of American Indian pottery have been found that have been exposed to rain for thousands of years. They still retain the shapes that the potter gave them.

▽▲▽▲▽▲▽▲▽▲▽▲▽▲▽▲▽▲▽▲▽▲▽▲▽▲▽

shatters easily. Clay dishes dissolve if they are placed in water or if water is placed in them. American Indian potters discovered that they could make their pottery stronger and hold water if they heated it in a fire instead of just letting it dry in the air.

When a potter places a shaped clay piece into a fire, the potter is really making a new kind of rock. Clay contains particles, or tiny pieces, of many kinds of minerals. The best clay for making pottery has minerals that contain the elements oxygen, hydrogen, silicon, and aluminum. When the clay is heated to a hot-enough temperature, some of the minerals melt. They undergo a chemical reaction. The oxygen atoms combine with the aluminum atoms, and the hydrogen atoms combine with the silicon atoms to form a hard, glasslike network. This framework holds the unmelted particles of clay in place. The hotter the fire the potter makes, the more kinds of minerals that melt and the harder and more waterproof the finished piece of pottery will be.

Making pottery was complex work. Potters first had to find deposits of clay that contained minerals that would melt in the fires that they built. American Indian potters needed to make fires as hot as 1,500 degrees Fahrenheit. Then they had to learn how to heat their pots to the right temperature without breaking them. They learned that if they mixed ground-up pieces of broken pots or ash from ancient volcanoes into the clay that they used, these materials would help to keep the clay from shattering when it was fired. They also found that if they let the fire die down completely before removing their pots, then the pots were less likely to break as they cooled.

MAKING DYES

American Indians invented many ways to dye, or color, fibers and leather. Often they used plant dyes to stain the material they were coloring. They made some of their dyes from berries and crushed flowers. They made other dyes by boiling the roots or bark of plants. American Indians of Mesoamerica, South America, and the Circum-Caribbean made red dye from tiny bugs called cochineal insects. They used mordants in order to make certain that the dyes would remain on whatever they were dying. A mordant is a metal salt, or alkali, that attaches to the protein molecules in fibers and to dye. It serves as a bridge to bond the fibers and dye together.

The Navajo used ashes boiled in water as a mordant to set dyes into fabric. The Blackfeet of the Plateau used ground cedar to set dyes. The tribes of the Plains used alkali soil as a mordant.

American Indians of Mesoamerica, the Caribbean, and the Southwest learned how to create a bright blue dye from the indigo

Aleutian basket weavers dyed beach grass that they used for making these baskets that were photographed in 1899. They gathered the grass after the Sun had bleached it. Light waves are composed of photons, which damage the molecules that give grass its color. The Aleutian Islands are a chain of islands that are part of Alaska. *(Library of Congress Prints and Photographs Division [LC-USZ62-101278])*

plant. The leaves of this plant contain a colorless chemical compound. The American Indians removed it from the plants' leaves by soaking them in water and letting them ferment. The fermenting produced a chemical reaction that changed the chemical compound into a sugar and a yellow liquid called indoxyl. American Indians stirred the yellow liquid so that it would be exposed to oxygen. When the indoxyl combined with oxygen, yet another chemical reaction took place—it turned blue and became a permanent dye.

ETCHING WITH ACID

The Hohokam, who lived in what is now Arizona starting in about 300 B.C., are thought to be the first people in the world to etch objects with acid. Etching uses acid to dissolve the surface layer of material. The Hohokam used this chemical process to make designs on shells.

Archaeologists believe that these American Indians fermented juice from the fruit of the saguaro cactus. This caused chemical changes in the juice. These changes produced acid. An acid is a sour-tasting solution that destroys the bonds between atoms in a base and creates a salt. (A base is any substance that reacts with an acid to form a salt.) Shells are made of calcium carbonate, which is a base. The acid that the Hohokam made was strong enough to dissolve shells by creating a salt where it touched them.

Hohokam people probably covered shells with pitch (sticky sap from trees) to protect parts of the shell from the acid. Then they scratched a design into the pitch. When they dipped the shells in the acid that they had made from cactus, the parts of the shell that were not coated with pitch dissolved. To stop the process, they washed the acid from the shells.

The Hohokam of the Southwest used acid to create designs on shells. They traded with other tribes for the shells. The Hohokam are thought to be the first people in the world to invent acid etching. *(E. B. Sayles, Photographer/Arizona State Museum, University of Arizona)*

ELECTROPLATING METALS

Moche metalworkers of South America made items made of various metals appear as if they were actually gold by electroplating them. They mixed water with potassium nitrate, salt, and alum to create a liquid that could dissolve gold. The metalworkers found these chemicals in their environment where they lived. When they combined them, the chemicals became a strong acid.

When the Moche metalworkers put gold into the acid solution, the gold began to dissolve and turn into a salt, a chemical formed by the combination of an acid and a base. The molecules, or clusters of atoms, that made up the gold salt had more protons than electrons. Protons are the parts of atoms that have a positive electrical charge. Electrons are the parts of atoms that have a negative charge. These two types of charges are equal and opposite. If an atom has more protons than electrons, it has a positive charge. The gold salt in the Moche electroplating solution had a positive charge.

Next the Moche metalworkers placed a copper object into the solution. The copper had more electrons than protons, so it had a negative electrical charge. This negative charge attracted the positively charged molecules of the gold salt. The gold salt was deposited on the surface of the copper to form a thin layer of gold. The metalworkers gently boiled the solution to speed this chemical reaction.

After they finished the electroplating, Moche metalworkers heated the object that they had plated to 900 to 940°F in order to make the bond between the gold and copper more permanent. Sometimes they electroplated objects with silver instead of gold. Europeans did not discover electroplating until the early 1800s.

TIME LINE	
9000 B.C. to 10,000 B.C.	Acorns become an important part of the diet of American Indians of California after they learn how to process them to remove tannins.
6000 B.C.	American Indians of the Amazon Basin learn how to fire clay to make pottery.
ca. 3000 B.C. to 2000 B.C.	People of the Amazon Basin domesticate manioc and learn to treat it so that it is safe to eat.
ca. A.D. 200	The Maya of Mesoamerica discover how to produce chocolate from cacao seeds.
ca. 200 B.C. to A.D. 600	The Moche people of what is now Peru use chemistry to electroplate metal.
A.D. 100 to A.D. 1100	The Hohokam people of the Southwest etch designs into shells with acid.

Math, Geometry, and Astronomy

American Indians understood the concept of numbers and named them. They knew how to count. Some groups of American Indians created numerals that they used for counting. A numeral is a written symbol that stands for a number. They organized numerals into number systems that had rules. These rules determined how numerals were to be written and what they stood for. Number systems also had rules for value and place. These rules allowed American Indians to make calculations, such as adding, subtracting, and, in some cases, multiplying.

American Indians used the numerals and number systems that they invented when they traded with other tribes. Indians of Mesoamerica used math when they bought and sold items in the marketplace. The Aztec of Mesoamerica developed standard weights and measures to make sure that business transactions were fair. They also used math to keep accounts and when they collected taxes. In South America, the Inca kept track of the number of people who lived in their empire and how much food and other goods that they had stored in warehouses.

In addition to using math for trading, buying, and selling, and accounting, American Indians used number systems to calculate the position and movement of the planets and stars. The Indian people of Mesoamerica invented calendars that they based on their math calculations. They used these calendars to predict where the planets and stars would appear in the sky in the future.

Indian people throughout the Americas used geometry to align their homes and religious buildings to the positions of the planets and stars at certain times of the year. American Indian builders also used geometry to plan the shapes of their buildings. Indian artisans used the principles of geometry to create designs for their blankets, pottery, clothing, and jewelry.

COUNTING AND NUMBER SYSTEMS

When people throughout the world first began to count, they used their fingers to help them. Some people used their fingers and their toes. Whatever a group of people used as a counting aid became the foundation, or basic unit of their system of counting.

Many groups of Indian people who lived in North America used a base 10 system for counting like the one that is used throughout the world today. The foundation of the base 10 system is the number of fingers on both hands. The levels of numbers in the base 10 system are ones, 10s, 100s (10×10), 1000s (100×100), and so on. The Algonquin- and Iroquoian-speaking peoples of the Northeast used a base 10 system for counting, as did the Athapascan-speaking people of the Arctic and Southwest and the Salish-speaking people of the Northwest. The Sioux (Dakota, Lakota, and Nakota) of the

NUMBERING SYSTEMS OF CALIFORNIA TRIBES

A small group of Yuki people, who lived in what is now Northern California, did not use their fingers as a foundation for their counting system. They used the spaces between their fingers to come up with a base 8 system of counting. They also used a base 16 system for counting. Sixteen is the number of spaces between the fingers and toes.

The Chumash people of what is now Southern California used a base 4 system and a base 16 number system. Some researchers believe that the base 4 system was based on the number of spaces between the fingers of one hand. The base 16 system was based on the number of spaces between the fingers of both hands and the number of spaces between the toes of each foot.

Maya Math System

The Olmec and Maya base 20 math system used only three symbols: dots, bars, and shells. A dot stood for one unit. A bar stood for five. A shell represented a zero. Later the Aztec used the same numbering system, but they substituted a drawing of an ear of corn for a shell. *(Facts On File)*

Great Plains also used a base 10 system. The Inca of South America used a base 10 system as well.

Mesoamerican Indians used a base 20 system. The Olmec are believed to have invented this system. An Olmec stone pillar with the equivalent of the date 31 B.C. written in Mesoamerican numerals is the oldest proof of a number system and a calendar in the Americas. The Olmec invented the zero between 1700 B.C. and 31 B.C. Zero is a numerical symbol that serves as a placeholder. Without a zero, both 203 and 23 would be written as 23. Besides preventing confusion, zero makes it possible to perform division. (Hindu mathematicians also invented the zero in about A.D. 595 in India.)

The Maya adopted the Olmec base 20 system and used it to perform complicated math problems and to make a very accurate calendar. The Aztec also used this system.

The first nine numerals in the Mesoamerican system were different. Combining the symbols for one through nine with the symbol for 10 formed the numerals 11 through 19. After that the numbers were organized in multiples of 20. The value of the bars and dots was determined by the positions in which they were written. Mesoamericans wrote the numerals vertically (up and down) instead of in a horizontal row. They wrote units in the bottom row. They wrote 20s on top of the units, and they wrote 400s on top of the 20s.

ACCOUNTING AND BUSINESS MATH

Many American Indians kept track of what they counted by keeping tallies. When people keep a tally, they make a mark to represent each thing that they are counting. Keeping a tally gives them a record of what they have counted, so that they do not have to remember the numbers. (Today people keep tallies as well. In a modern tally that people use when they play a game and want to keep score, [卌 IIII] stands for nine things.) American Indians used tallies to keep score when they raced or played dice games. They also kept tallies to count the number of people in their

▲▽▲▽▲▽▲▽▲▽▲▽▲▽▲▽▲▽▲▽▲▽▲▽▲▽▲

MEASURING MONEY

The Pomo people, who lived in what is now California, used beads for money. They made the beads from clamshells that they cut into disks and drilled with a center hole. The Pomo made shell money so that each bead was the same thickness and had the same diameter. Pomo traders kept the beads on strings. Because the beads were all the same, the traders could measure the string to determine its value instead of stopping to count the beads. The Pomo used a base 20 number system.

▽▲▽▲▽▲▽▲▽▲▽▲▽▲▽▲▽▲▽▲▽▲▽▲▽▲▽

Maya traders loaded rafts with goods such as dye, cotton cloth, and chocolate. They traveled up and down the east coast of Mesoamerica and to trade with Indians of the Caribbean. Math was important to them as traders. This picture of a fishing raft similar to the rafts that the Maya traders used was made in 1565. *(Library of Congress Prints and Photographs Division [LC-USZ62-71995])*

▲▽▲▽▲▽▲▽▲▽▲▽▲▽▲▽▲▽▲▽▲▽▲▽▲▽▲▽▲▽▲

MEASURING LAND

Aztec rulers collected taxes from the people who lived in their empire. In order to figure how much tax people needed to pay, the Aztec had to find a way to accurately measure the land on which they lived. The unit that they used to measure fields was called the square *quahuitl*. It was about 1.09 yards long on each side. Tax collectors measured the sides of the fields with ropes to find the perimeter. They calculated the area from these measurements.

▼▲▼▲▼▲▼▲▼▲▼▲▼▲▼▲▼▲▼▲▼▲▼▲▼▲▼▲▼▲▼

CVRACA·CON DOR·CHAVA

The Inca used quipus to record information. Some experts on the quipu have compared this way of storing information to the binary system used by today's computers. The lower left corner of this picture shows a *yupana*, an Inca counting box. (After Felipe Guamán Poma de Ayala. Nueva corónica y buen gobierno)

tribe and when they traded goods with other groups of Indian people.

In addition to using tallies, some American Indians discovered other ways to help them quickly add and subtract with accuracy. Maya merchants used cacao beans or other counters arranged on a flat surface to do math problems in the marketplace. They subtracted by taking counters from the proper row. They added by placing more counters in the proper row.

Maya and Aztec merchants also used an abacus to solve math problems. An abacus is a frame with rods or strings that are strung with counters. The Aztec called the Mesoamerican abacus a *nepohualtzitzin*. They strung it with dry maize, or corn kernels. This abacus had three kernels on the top deck and four kernels on the bottom. Archaeologists (scientists who study the past) believe that the Maya began using these counters between A.D. 900 and A.D. 1000.

The Inca, whose empire was established in what is now Peru in about A.D. 1000, also had a type of abacus that they called a *yupana*. It was a tray with compartments, or boxes. The compartments were arranged in rows. To add and subtract, the Inca moved the counters from compartment to compartment. They used pebbles, beans, or corn for markers.

The Inca used scales to weigh items. The scales were made by hanging small pans or net bags on each end of a stick. The merchant held the stick in the middle and placed the material to be weighed at one end. Then the merchant placed stone weights on the other side until the scales balanced.

The people of the Andes Mountains of South America invented a way to keep track of hundreds of different numbers. Between about A.D. 600 and A.D. 1000 they invented the quipu, a group of colored knotted strings, to store this information. The first people to use quipus were llama herders, who tied knots in string to keep track of their animals. The number and type of knots that they tied into the strings stood for different numbers. The color of the strings and where they tied the knots also had special meanings. The higher the knot was tied on the string, the higher the number that it represented. (The highest number a quipu could record was 10,000.) Ones were tied at the bottom.

Today more is known about the Inca quipu than those used by earlier people of the Andes. Inca quipus often had more than 100 individual knotted strings of many colors. These were tied to a main string. The Inca used quipus to record the number of people and goods in their empire. In the Inca Empire, a person who had been trained in how to make and read a quipu was called a *quipucamayoc*. After this person had tied the knots on the quipu strings, runners, called *chasqui*, carried the quipu in relays along the Inca road system. When the quipu reached its destination another *quipucamayoc* translated the meaning of the knots.

GEOMETRY

Geometry studies and measures the relationships between points, lines, and angles. American Indians used geometry to shape their homes and plan their cities. Indian builders of Mesoamerica and South America used geometry to plan pyramids. The Anasazi of the Southwest needed to understand geometry in order to build kivas, round rooms where they held ceremonies. They built these kivas starting between A.D. 700 and A.D. 900. American Indians also used geometry to create designs on buildings, pottery, and cloth.

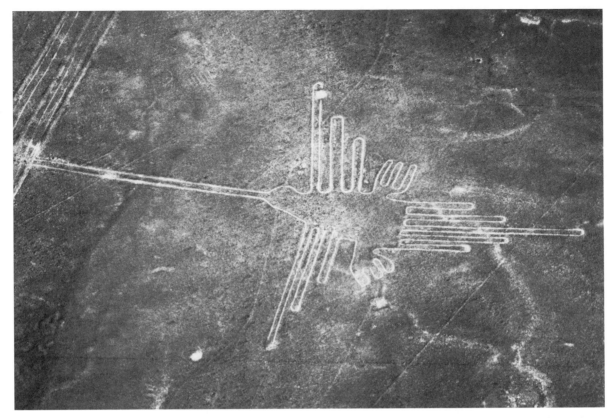

The Nazca made huge geometrical designs on the desert in what is now Peru. Nazca culture flourished from about 900 B.C. to A.D. 600. These mysterious figures are so large that they can only be viewed from the air. They could not have been created without planning and a knowledge of geometry. *(© Philip Baird/www.anthroarchear.org)*

To build round earth lodges, the Omaha of the Great Plains first needed to draw a very large circle on the ground. To do this they drove a wooden stake into the place that would be the center of their home. Then they tied a long cord to the stake. After stretching the cord, they would tie another stick to the free end of the cord. By walking and scratching the stick on the ground, they could make a perfect circle.

Aztec builders used the same method to make circles. They called this compass a *tlayolloanaloni* in the Aztec language, Nahuatl. They used a *temetzetepilolli*, a plumb made from a weight tied to a string, to make a straight vertical (up and down) line. Aztec and Maya builders also used a level, called a *quamniztli*, and a square to create right angles.

To make certain that floor plans of their wooden homes were square, the Kwakiutl of the Pacific Northwest used a rope that they had made from cedar bark to mark the distance from what would be the center of the front door to what would be the center of the back door. Then they folded the rope back on itself so that they would have a measurement for half of this distance. They used this measurement to pound two stakes as closely as they could get to a

The Navajo use geometric designs when they weave their rugs. They also use symmetry. One half of the rug looks like the mirror image of the other half. *(Library of Congress, Prints and Photographs Division [LC-USZ62-113860])*

90-degree (right) angle to the front door stake. This marked the two front corners of the house. Finally they used a rope to measure the distance between each front corner and the rear door stake. If the measurements were the same, they had made right angles. If the measurements turned out to be unequal, they adjusted the stakes until they were equal.

Archaeologists were slow to recognize that American Indians understood geometry. One reason for this is that many groups of American Indians based their geometry on the circle. Another reason is that often the buildings that the archaeologists studied were so old that their walls had shifted. A final reason for their confusion is that American Indian builders often aligned parts of their buildings to the rising and setting of planets or star constellations. This required an understanding of geometry, math, and astronomy.

American Indian art is filled with geometric designs. Mesoamerican designers used patterns and templates for sculpture and painting. In addition to the ability to create nearly perfect right angles, American Indian artists understood symmetry. A design that has symmetry is a design that is repeated on both sides of a central axis, or line. The designs on Pueblo pottery and in Navajo (Dineh) rugs and beadwork of Plains tribes are further examples of geometry.

ASTRONOMY

Astronomy is the study of the position and movement of planets, stars, and constellations (groups of stars). American Indians in North America, Mesoamerica, and South America focused on events that happened at the horizon, the line where the sky and Earth appear to meet. These events included the rising and setting of the Sun and the Moon. American Indian astronomers paid special attention to the rising and setting of the planet Venus as well. They also kept track of the winter and summer solstices as well as the spring and fall equinoxes. (The winter solstice is the shortest day of the year, and the summer solstice is the longest. On the two equinoxes, day and night are of equal length.)

To help them in their observations, American Indian astronomers built pillars as pointers to places in the sky where important events happened at certain times during the year. They also built walls with windows that framed important events during special times during the year. Some of these ancient astronomers kept records of what they saw in the sky, and they used the information that they gathered to create calendars, systems to mark the passing of time. Mesoamerican Indians made elaborate calendars by using math to calculate when events such as solar eclipses would happen again.

Rocks that Indian astronomers arranged into the shape of wheels are the oldest evidence of calendars in North America. Many of these wheels have been found throughout the northern plains of the United States and Canada. Today they are called medicine wheels. American Indians built them on high hills or bluffs that gave a clear view of the sky. The oldest medicine wheels are in what are now Montana and Saskatchewan. The stone spokes of these medicine wheels, which radiate out from the center point, align to the rising of stellar, or star, constellations at the time of the summer solstice. The Bighorn medicine wheel in what is now Montana is thought to be many hundreds of years old. Parts of this wheel align with the sunrise at the summer solstice. Other parts of the Bighorn medicine wheel are aligned to the rising of the constellations Aldebaran and

This picture of the medicine wheel in the Big Horn Mountains near Sheridan, Wyoming, was taken in 1917. The medicine wheel is about 75 feet in diameter and has 28 spokes that radiate from the center. Today it is a National Historic Landmark. Between 70 and 150 similar wheels have been found in Montana, Wyoming, South Dakota, Alberta, and Saskatchewan. *(Denver Public Library, Western History Collection/Photo. Herbert H. Thompson/No. X-32076)*

Sirius. A medicine wheel at Moose Mountain in Canada has similar alignments to those of the Big Horn medicine wheel. It is believed to be about 2,600 years old.

The Anasazi, whose culture arose in the desert southwest of what is now the United States in about 350 B.C. and lasted until about A.D. 1300, built Casa Rinaconada, a kiva, in about A.D. 1100. This round building, which they used for religious ceremonies, has windows and

▲▼▲▼▲▼▲▼▲▼▲▼▲▼▲▼▲▼▲▼▲▼▲▼▲▼▲▼▲▼▲▼▲▼▲▼▲▼▲

AN AMERICAN INDIAN ASTRONAUT

John Bennett Herrington, a commander in the U.S. Navy, is the first American Indian to become an astronaut. Herrington, who is a member of the Chickasaw tribe, has been interested in space for as long as he can remember. He used to pretend that a cardboard box was his spaceship when he was a boy.

His family had moved 14 times by the time he graduated from high school in Plano, Texas. He started college but earned low grades and dropped out. Herrington did not give up. He enrolled in school again. In 1983 he earned a bachelor of science degree in applied mathematics from the University of Colorado at Colorado Springs.

He enlisted in the U.S. Navy and became an officer the year after he graduated. In the navy Herrington flew planes and eventually became a test pilot. He earned a master's degree in science in 1995. In 1996 he was selected to be an astronaut by the National Aeronautics and Space Administration (NASA).

Herrington flew on the *Endeavor*, the 16th space shuttle to visit the Interna-

Astronaut John Bennett Herrington is a member of the Chickasaw tribe. The Chickasaw people lived in what are now Alabama, Kentucky, and Tennessee. Their lands were taken by the British during the Revolutionary War. They lived with the Creek until the Indian Removal Act of 1830 when they moved to Indian Territory (now Oklahoma). *(Courtesy of National Aeronautics and Space Administration)*

▼▲▼▲▼▲▼▲▼▲▼▲▼▲▼▲▼▲▼▲▼▲▼▲▼▲▼▲▼▲▼▲▼▲▼▲▼▲▼

niches, or indentations, which modern astronomers have found are aligned with the light of the summer solstice.

The Anasazi also built a calendar at Chaco Canyon in what is now New Mexico. They arranged large rock slabs atop a high butte, or flat-topped hill, so that shafts of sunlight fell between them on a carving of a spiral drawn onto a cliff. As the angle of the sunlight changed with the seasons, shafts of light fell on different parts of the

John Bennett Herrington takes time out from his busy schedule aboard the space shuttle Endeavor on a mission to repair the International Space Station. *(Courtesy of National Aeronautics and Space Administration)*

tional Space Station in 2002. On his journey into space, he carried the Chickasaw flag, an eagle feather, and an arrowhead with him. During the mission he performed three space walks outside of the shuttle. During these space walks, he and another astronaut worked on the outside of the space station.

Herrington is a member of the American Indian Science and Engineering Society. He travels throughout the country encouraging American Indian students to become scientists and to aim for the stars when they set their goals.

In this painting, the artist imagines how Woodhenge would have looked when the Mississippian Indians built this giant calendar sometime between A.D. 900 and A.D. 1100. *(Painting by L. K. Townsend, Courtesy of Cahokia Mounds State Historic Site)*

carving. This enabled people who knew how to read the stone calendar to tell important dates. Called the Sun Dagger Calendar, it is at least 700 years old.

The Hopi people of the Southwest used the landscape as a horizon calendar for centuries. They timed their annual ceremonies to the position of the Sun as it rose over what are now called the San Francisco Peaks. The notches and mesas of these mountains served as markers. By watching the sky and noting the rising and setting positions of the Sun and Moon, the Hopi could tell when crops were ready to plant. Modern experiments have shown that by using these predictions, Hopi farmers could avoid freezing crops with great accuracy.

The American Indians of Cahokia created a huge calendar that is called Woodhenge today. It was given this name because it reminded archaeologists of the Stonehenge standing stones in England.

Mesoamerican calendars were very accurate. By about 2,500 years ago, American Indian astronomers had figured a year's length so accurately that it was only 19 minutes off. This mosaic is a copy of an Aztec calendar. *(Neg. No. 315090. Photo Rice & Bierwert. Courtesy of Library Services, American Museum of Natural History)*

This building, called the Caracol, in Chichén Itzá is an example of a Maya building with windows that are aligned to the stars and planets. Chichén Itzá, an important Maya culture center, was built during the early 900s. The building once had a lower and an upper tower on a high stone platform. The roof of the upper tower had a large opening that could have been used to observe the sky. *(© Philip Baird/www.anthroarchear.org)*

Cahokia, located near the site of modern St. Louis, was the largest city built by the people of the Mississippian culture. They built Woodhenge between A.D. 900 and A.D. 1100. Today it consists of large, oval-shaped pits. They once contained posts that were arranged in as many as five circles. These were aligned to the position of the Sun at equinoxes and solstices. Each circle had a center post where an astronomer may have stood to observe sunrises on the eastern horizon.

Both the Sun and the constellation Pleiades marked the planting season for agricultural people in North America. Seneca communities living in what is now New York State observed that the constellation Pleiades rose by the middle of October, and they timed their midwinter ceremony to occur when the constellation was directly above them. They planted their corn, a variety that requires 120 frost-free days, when the Pleiades disappeared below the horizon in mid-May. The Sac (Sauk), Mesquaki, and the Dakota, Lakota, and Nakota people of the Great Plains all have legends about this constellation. The Lakota people timed their religious ceremonies according to where certain constellations appeared in the sky. The Pawnee of the Great Plains watched the moving planets and constellations through the smoke holes in the roofs of their earth lodges.

Maya astronomers of Mesoamerica used buildings, such as temples, when they observed the planets and stars at the horizon. They measured their movement by looking at the sky through sticks crossed at right angles. Sirius, the brightest star in the sky after the Sun, was important to Mesoamerican astronomers, as was the planet Venus. The Maya used the movements of the stars and planets to plan buildings and cities. They also used these movements to make calendars and almanacs, books that contained information about the planets and stars.

The Maya created several calendars, which the Aztec later used. Each of them served a different purpose. The day count was a 260-day almanac that they used to plan religious ceremonies, name children, and predict the future. The Maya also kept a yearly calendar based on the Sun. It contained 365 days that were arranged into 18 months. Each month had 20 days. The Maya, and later the Aztec, used this calendar to plan market gatherings and crop plantings. In addition to the solar calendar, the Maya devised a lunar calendar. This calendar consisted of alternating periods of 29 and 30 days in order to compensate for the actual time it took for one lunar cycle to complete.

▲▽▲▽▲▽▲▽▲▽▲▽▲▽▲▽▲▽▲▽▲▽▲▽▲▽▲▽▲

AN ACCURATE CALENDAR

Without using telescopes, the Maya calculated a year's length so precisely that it was only 19 minutes off. The scientific tools these ancient astronomers used were shadow-casting devices, accurate observation, and very careful record keeping.

▽▲▽▲▽▲▽▲▽▲▽▲▽▲▽▲▽▲▽▲▽▲▽▲▽▲▽▲▽

The Inca of South America also watched the skies. They built stone pillars to mark the spring equinoxes so that farmers would know when to plant crops. Many of these pillars were located around the Inca capital city of Cuzco. The pillars were so large that they could be seen from about nine miles away. Two of these pillars marked where the Sun set during the summer solstice, the longest day of the year. The Inca year began when the constellation Pleiades rose on the horizon. Phases of the Moon determined the dates that the Inca set for their religious festivals. To measure the passage of short periods of time when accuracy was not important, the Inca used the time it took to boil a potato, a vegetable that Indian people of the Andes Mountains raised.

TIME LINE

3000 B.C.	Ancient builders at El Aspero in what is now Peru use geometry to plan their pyramids.
1700 B.C. to 31 B.C.	The Olmec of Mesoamerica invent the zero.
1500 B.C.	Olmec builders use geometry to plan and build pyramids.
600 B.C. to 500 B.C.	The Maya of Mesoamerica invent the day calendar.
600 B.C.	North American Indians of the Great Plains begin building stone medicine wheels.
A.D. 600 to A.D. 1000	American Indians of the Andes Mountains invent the quipu.
A.D. 900 to A.D. 1000	The Maya of Mesoamerica invent the abacus.
A.D. 900 to A.D. 1100	Mississippian people of North America build Woodhenge at Cahokia.

Civil Engineering

Civil engineers use their knowledge of science and technology to plan and build large public projects for the common good. These projects include dams, roads, and large public buildings. Indians of the Americas built complex water systems, roads, earthworks, and pyramids. These projects took a great deal of planning and often took them many years to build.

AMERICAN INDIAN ENGINEERS OF NORTH AMERICA

American Indians who lived in what is now Florida dug canals to make travel from one place to another more efficient. The oldest known canals were dug about 1,700 years ago. The Indians located them at the site of an earthen mound near what is now the Caloosahatchee River, about 15 miles west of Lake Okeechobee. The mound was the center of a village where about 200 to 300 people once lived. The village was a part of a settlement of many villages.

The canals are three to four feet deep and 20 feet wide. One of them is seven miles long. These ancient canals allowed Indian people who lived in the village to travel between the lake and the Gulf of Mexico without having to go through rapids in the river. The Indian engineers, who had to remove millions of cubic yards of soil, dug the canals with tools that they made from wood and shells.

Archaeologists have found many more ancient canals near Lake Okeechobee. Some of these canals had lock systems, compartments built into a canal that can be flooded and drained in order to raise or lower the water level. The locks enabled canoes to travel uphill. About 40 canals in the area were built in circular shapes and have drainage ditches extending from them. The oldest of these may have been built as early as 450 B.C. Scientists believe that the circular

73

canals may have been used to drain land for farming. Others think that the canals may have been giant ponds where the people raised fish for food.

The canals that Indian people of Florida built extended to both coasts and crossed the Everglades, the swampy lowland of central Florida. The people who built the canals were traders who may have traveled as far away as the Ohio River Valley in their dugout canoes in order to exchange goods.

American Indians of the swamps, coastline, and keys of what is now Florida also built huge piles of shells. (Keys are low islands.) These shell mounds made swampy ground more solid. Some archaeologists believe that the early Indians of Florida Keys built houses on the shells and planted gardens in the mud-filled spaces between the shell heaps.

By the middle of the 1500s the Calusa Indians of Florida had built many shell mounds. They even built an island that is called Mound Key today. The place where they built Mound Key was covered with water during high tide. The Calusa began this project by driving the pointed ends of large shells into the sandy ocean bottom just off the coast. They used these conch and whelk shells to create a solid foundation. Next they gathered marl from the bottoms of lakes that had high mineral content. Marl is a grayish-white sediment, or deposit, of calcium carbonate that hardens like cement when it settles or dries. The Indian engineers packed marl around the foundation shells

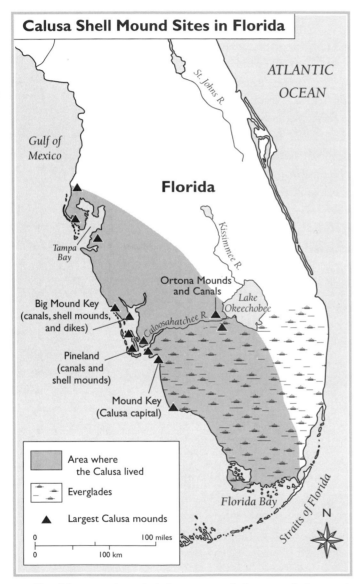

Calusa Shell Mound Sites in Florida

ATLANTIC OCEAN

St. Johns R.

Gulf of Mexico

Florida

Kissimmee R.

Tampa Bay

Ortona Mounds and Canals

Lake Okeechobee

Big Mound Key (canals, shell mounds, and dikes)

Caloosahatchee R.

Pineland (canals and shell mounds)

Mound Key (Calusa capital)

Straits of Florida

Florida Bay

Area where the Calusa lived

Everglades

Largest Calusa mounds

0   100 miles
0   100 km

N

The Calusa people and their ancestors built many shell mounds and canals in the southwest part of what is now Florida. This map shows only the largest ones.

they had driven into the sand and waited for it to harden. Then they added more layers of marl and soil to raise the level of the island. The Calusa also made seawalls from large pointed shells and marl to keep large waves from carrying away sand and eroding the shoreline of the Gulf Coast.

The Anasazi people, who lived in what are now Arizona, New Mexico,

CANALS TO IRRIGATE THE DESERT

In the desert Southwest, Hohokam people built canals to bring water to fields where they grew cotton, corn, and beans. They began digging these canals before A.D. 300 along the Salt and Gila River Valleys in what is now Phoenix, Arizona. During the next 500 years they built more than 150 miles of canals. Some of them were more than 30 feet wide and many were more than 10 feet deep. These American Indian engineers plastered the sides of the canals and designed them so that gravity would move the water where they needed it to go.

The Hopi, who are considered the descendants of the Anasazi, built terraced fields on the walls of the mesas where they have lived in what is now Arizona since about A.D. 1100. (A mesa is a hill with steep sides and a flat top.) Natural springs on top of the mesas provided water for crops that the Hopi planted. This old etching shows the Hopi village of Walpi, where Hopi people have lived continuously since about A.D. 1200. *(U.S. Bureau of Ethnography)*

By the time non-Indian farmers arrived in the Mississippi and Ohio River Valleys, Indian mounds had been abandoned for hundreds of years. Farmers mistook some of them for natural hills and planted crops on them. When they recognized mounds as burial sites, they dug for "treasure." Many people mistakenly believed that ancient people who were unrelated to American Indians had built the mounds. *(Photograph No. NWDNS-106-N-INE-5, National Archives and Records Administration—College Park)*

Utah, and Colorado, built systems of terraces and small dams to water their fields between 1000 A.D. and 1200 A.D. In Mesa Verde, a large Anasazi settlement in the southwest of what is now Colorado,

archaeologists discovered hundreds of such dams after a 1996 fire cleared plants and trees from a national park there. The Anasazi at Mesa Verde also built reservoirs to store water for their crops and homes.

In addition to building canals, the Anasazi people built roads. In Chaco Canyon in what is now New Mexico, they built a road system that linked outlying settlements to the main community, Casa Bonita. These roads were straight and radiated from the canyon like spokes on a wheel. The longest Anasazi road in Chaco Canyon was 42 miles long.

Mound building Indians of the Northeast and Southeast created thousands of earthworks in the United States and the southern part of Canada. They used shovels and hoes made of clamshells and wood to collect soil for these earthworks. They also used the shoulder blades of large animals, such as buffalo, as building tools. They carried the dirt in baskets to where they were building a mound.

The Adena, who lived in the Mississippi and Ohio River Valleys beginning in about B.C. 1500 were the first to build mounds in North America. At first they began making small mounds of earth as burial sites. Over time, they buried more people in the mounds that they had made, and the cone-shaped mounds grew higher. Adena culture began to fade in about A.D. 200.

Serpent Mound in Ohio is the largest effigy mound in the United States. It is four to five feet high and 1,330 feet long. Its width varies between 20 and 25 feet. Some archaeologists believe it was built by the Adena people in about 500 B.C. Recent evidence shows that it might have been built as late as A.D. 950–1200. *(Library of Congress, Prints and Photographs Division [LC-USZ62-049402])*

The Hopewell were the next people to build mounds, from about 300 B.C. to about A.D. 700. Like the Adena, they lived in the Mississippi and Ohio River Valleys. The Hopewell built much larger earthen mounds than the Adena did. They were skilled craftspeople, who made beautiful objects that they buried with the dead in the mounds that they built. These objects included jewelry, precious stones, and shells. They were also known as traders. Hopewell engineers built a perfectly straight 60-mile-long road linking two of their communities.

Beginning in about A.D. 600, some groups of Indians in the upper Midwest began making mounds in the shape of birds and animals. These are called effigy mounds. Some of the mounds that they built were shaped like bears, bison, eagles, or lizards. These mounds were very large. A bear-shaped mound in Effigy Mounds National Monument in Iowa is 137 feet long and 3$^{1}/_{2}$ feet tall. Another bear is about 80 feet long and 2$^{1}/_{2}$ feet high. The people who built effigy mounds rarely used them for burials.

The last Indians to build mounds were those of the Mississippian culture, which lasted from about A.D. 800 to about 1500. Mississippian Indians built the largest mounds in North America. Some of these mounds were about the size of football fields. The biggest Mississippian mounds were flat on top. They served as platforms for temples and the homes of rulers, which were built on top of them. Mississippian people buried their dead in smaller, cone-shaped mounds.

The largest group of Mississippian mounds is at Cahokia. Built near the modern city of St. Louis, Missouri, Cahokia was once the largest city in North America. It covered about 4,000 acres. About 20,000 people lived there. Ancient American Indian engineers designed and made 120 mounds at Cahokia. To build them, they dug and carried more than 50 million cubic feet of earth. The entire city was surrounded by a stockade, a fence made of about 20,000 logs.

Cahokia's largest mound is named Monks Mound. (It is called this because it was the site of a Trappist monastery in the early 1800s.) This enormous mound contains about 22 million cubic feet of earth and covers 14 acres at its base. It is 48 feet wide, 105 feet long and about 50 feet tall at its highest point. Monks Mound has several terraces that the people of Cahokia built in several stages between A.D. 900 and 1200.

Monks Mound is the largest earthwork in the United States that American Indian people built. It is about 92 feet high and was made up of four terraces. The Indians who built it in A.D. 950 first made a clay core. Then they covered it with alternating layers of pebbles, sandy soil, and clay to drain rainfall from the mound so that it would not collapse. *(Courtesy of Cahokia Mounds State Historic Site)*

AMERICAN INDIAN ENGINEERS
OF MESOAMERICA

Mesoamerican Indians were also master engineers. The Olmec, whose culture arose in about 1500 B.C. in the southern part of what is now Mexico, used stone tools to build water channels out of basalt, a volcanic rock that is very hard and heavy. Olmec stoneworkers carved basalt into U-shaped containers and laid them end to end in ditches that ran from water sources to the places that needed water. They set the stone in place with clay and covered the channels with stone lids that they had carved.

The Maya, whose culture arose in about 1500 B.C., built small fields that were surrounded by canals. These raised garden plots are

The Aztec used *chinampas,* or artificial islands, to grow crops that fed the people of the Aztec capital of Tenochtitlán (now Mexico City). About 250,000 people lived in this city, which was located in the central part of what is now Mexico. This picture was taken in about 1931 at Xochimilco, south of Mexico City. The *chinampas* that remain today are used to grow flowers for tourists. *(Library of Congress, Prints and Photographs Division [LC-USZ62-121397])*

called *chinampas.* To make the artificial islands, first they drained swamps and shallow lakes by digging long straight ditches to clear them of as much water as possible. Next they dug canals in the land that they had drained and piled soil in mounds to form garden plots. When they had finished, they refilled the canals with water. They built *chinampas* four to five feet above the waterline so that the roots of their crops did not get too much water. Maya engineers anchored the soil in place by planting small trees along the edges of the islands that they had made.

The Aztec made *chinampas* by hauling canoe loads of sod from the mainland and depositing them in shallow Lakes Chalco and Xochimilco. By A.D. 1200, they had covered large areas of both lakes with artificial islands. By the 1500s, these agricultural plots nearly covered the lakes. The Aztec used the canals between the *chinampas* to transport the food grown there to markets in the cities that surrounded these lakes.

Aztec engineers converted Lake Texcoco from a saltwater lake into a freshwater lake. They did this by building a network of gated dikes, or dams, and aqueducts (raised water channels) that were fed by a freshwater spring. The largest dike was almost 10 miles long. The Aztec built it sometime after A.D. 1440 to keep salt water from flooding the *chinampas* and the Aztec capital city of Tenochtitlán. Water that has a high salt content kills plants and is not good for drinking. The Aztec used the tops of their dikes as roads.

Ancient engineers of Mesoamerica built many other roads as well. The Olmec were the first Mesoamericans to build unpaved roads. Olmec roads and trails later became the foundation for Maya roads. Maya engineers built low walls on each side of the road and filled them with stone slabs. They covered the slabs with gravel to surface the road. Maya road builders covered some of their roads with cement. The road network that they built crossed the Yucatán Peninsula. Later the Aztec used Maya roads.

From 1878 to 1923 the U.S. government sent many American Indian young people to Hampton Normal and Agricultural Institute, a school established to train freed slaves to become teachers. The goal of Indian education at this time was to make American Indians part of the non-Indian world. They were not allowed to speak their own languages and were not taught about American Indian accomplishments. In this picture that was taken in 1899, an American Indian student (middle row) learns about Egyptian pyramids in an ancient culture class. *(Library of Congress, Prints and Photographs Division [LC-USZ62-59189])*

The Maya, who were traders, also traveled by ocean. They built seaport towns along the coast in areas with bays that were protected from storms and high waves. Maya engineers built docks and piers in these ports. They even built a sea wall at Cerritos to form an artificial harbor.

In addition to canals, roads, and harbors, Mesoamerican Indians engineered pyramids. The Olmec began building pyramids between 2000 and 1500 B.C. One of the largest, at La Venta, stood 112 feet high. Olmec engineers built rooms on each level, or tier, and then filled them in with rock, sand, and gravel. When all the rooms were full, they built another level. They filled it and repeated the process until the pyramid was completed. The ancient engineers then used basalt or granite to build an outer surface, called a facing, on their pyramids.

The Maya, who used building techniques that had been invented by the Olmec, built the largest pyramid in Mesoamerica. It was located at Cholula, in what are now the Mexican highlands.

The Inca stored water for their fields in reservoirs.
(After Felipe Guamán Poma de Ayala. Nueva corónica y buen gobierno)

This pyramid stood 181 feet high and was part of a complex that covered an area of at least 25 acres. The Aztec also built pyramids in the Mesoamerican tradition that the Olmec had begun.

AMERICAN INDIAN ENGINEERS OF SOUTH AMERICA

In South America, farmers living in the Andes Mountains of what is now Peru began using a system of small raised fields separated by canals in about 300 B.C. Farmers of the plains of what are now Peru and Bolivia used this method as well. It helped them to produce large amounts of food crops even though they lived in an area that flooded often. They called this way of farming *waru waru.*

Long before the Inca Empire was established, Indian people who lived in what is now Peru planted crops on the steep slopes of valleys because valleys received more rainfall than flatter land did. These farmers leveled small plots of land for their crops. They used large

▲▼▲▼▲▼▲▼▲▼▲▼▲▼▲▼▲▼▲▼▲▼▲▼▲

ENGINEERS OF THE AMAZON RAIN FOREST

Farmers in the rain forest of the Xinguano region of what is now Brazil built raised fields that were surrounded by ditches full of water between A.D. 1250 and 1600. Archaeologists have found the remains of a group of at least 19 towns. The people who lived there built ditches and canals to control the water for their orchards and manioc fields. (Manioc is a starchy, root vegetable.) The Xinguano people, whose work shows a knowledge of mathematics, astronomy, and engineering, created 16-feet-deep ditches around the villages. They also built ponds, bridges, and straight roads with curbs between their villages. Some of the roads were causeways. Causeways are roads raised above swamps or water. From 2,500 people to 5,000 Xinguano people lived in clusters of six to 12 villages.

▼▲▼▲▼▲▼▲▼▲▼▲▼▲▼▲▼▲▼▲▼▲▼▲▼

blocks of limestone to hold the soil so that it would not wash down the steep slopes during rainstorms. Terraced farming was so successful that farmers of the Andes eventually abandoned *waru waru* farming. By about A.D. 1000, shortly before the Inca Empire was established, hundreds of acres of terraces surrounded the Inca capital city of Cuzco.

The Moche, who lived on the northern coast of what is now Peru from 200 B.C. to A.D. 600, were also skilled water engineers. They built miles of irrigation ditches and stone aqueducts that crossed valleys. An aqueduct that they built in the Chicama Valley was nearly 50 feet high and a mile long.

Later, the Inca, who established their empire about A.D. 1100, controlled water in the same area by building narrow canals and ditches. They regulated the water flow with stone gates. Inca engineers straightened streams and paved their beds. The Inca used water to irrigate their fields and channeled it into cities to use for drinking and bathing.

The Inca are best known for the road system that they built. Inca engineers built two main roads that ran north and south through

Inca builders created many large public buildings. They cut huge stones and fit them into place so well that many of these buildings remain standing today. The round building in this picture is the Temple of the Sun. It was built at Machu Picchu, an Inca city high in the Andes Mountains of what is now Peru. At one time its walls were covered with gold. (© *Philip Baird/w.w.w.anthroarchear.org*)

▲▽▲▽▲▽▲▽▲▽▲▽▲▽▲▽▲▽▲▽▲▽▲▽▲▽▲▽▲▽▲

THE FIRST PYRAMID BUILDERS

South American Indian engineers began building pyramids several hundred years before the Egyptians began building their pyramids. Archaeologists believe that the Egyptians built their first pyramid at Saqqara between 2886 B.C. and 2613 B.C. They constructed the famous pyramids at Giza between 2589 B.C. and 2504 B.C.

▽▲▽▲▽▲▽▲▽▲▽▲▽▲▽▲▽▲▽▲▽▲▽▲▽▲▽▲▽▲▽

their empire. One was in the highlands and the other ran along the Pacific coast from what is now northern Ecuador to southern Chile. A number of smaller roads that branched from the main one connected villages. Inca roads varied in width from 82 feet where the ground was flat to very narrow stretches that they carved into solid rock. The narrow roads zig-zagged up mountain slopes.

Inca engineers carved tunnels through hills. They lined some of these tunnels with stone. They also built causeways. One causeway was eight miles long. The Inca built causeways of packed earth and covered the earth with stone slabs. Sometimes they surfaced the causeways with soil with high levels of calcium carbonate that acted like cement.

The Inca built several types of bridges. Some of these bridges were cantilevered. Cantilevered bridges are anchored at one end. The Inca built pontoon bridges that floated on the water. They also built suspension bridges to cross deep valleys in the mountains. They hung these bridges on fiber ropes that they strung between huge poles. One of the suspension bridges that Inca engineers made was 200 feet long.

The ancient Indian people of what is now Peru were the first in the Americas to build pyramids. They began building them from adobe (sun-dried mud) in about 3000 B.C. One of the first of these pyramids was at El Aspero, located in the central coastal area of present-day Peru. This settlement covered 33 acres.

The Huaca del Sol, built by Moche engineers in what is now Peru, is known as the largest adobe structure in the Americas that Indian people built before Europeans arrived. The base of the Huaca del Sol pyramid is 1,132 feet by 525 feet. The pyramid stands 98 feet tall. Archaeologists believe that the builders had to shape about 140 million adobe bricks and then lay them in place to create it.

TIME LINE	
3000 B.C.	Ancient people of what is now Peru begin building pyramids.
1500 B.C.	Mesoamerican engineers start building *chinampas* from earth. They plant crops on these human-made islands located in swamps and shallow lakes.
200 B.C. to A.D. 600	Moche people of what is now Peru build a large system of irrigation ditches and stone aqueducts.
A.D. 200 to 700	Ancient builders living in what is now Florida dig a network of canals that they use for transportation.
A.D. 300 to 800	Hohokam builders dig 150 miles of canals in the desert of what is now Arizona in order to provide water for their crops.
A.D. 1000 to A.D. 1200	The Anasazi, who live in the southwest part of what is now Colorado, build hundreds of small dams that divert rainwater to their crops. They also build a road system at Chaco Canyon.
A.D. 1100	Inca engineers begin to build roads and bridges throughout their South American empire.
A.D. 1250	Xinguaneo engineers build ditches, canals, roads and bridges in the Amazon rain forest.
A.D. 1440 to A.D. 1450	The Aztec plan and build a 10-mile-long dike across lake Texcoco, which they change from a saltwater lake to a freshwater lake.

Writing

Writing is a way to preserve and share information by making marks on a surface such as rock or paper. These marks can be letters, or they can be a system of pictures or symbols that are understood by a number of people besides the person who wrote them. Indian people throughout the Americas used a writing system called pictograms to record information. Pictograms are symbols that illustrate an idea or object.

The standard symbols that represent men and women that are posted on the doors of public restrooms are examples of modern pictograms. Other modern pictograms are road signs showing rocks falling onto the road and care labels on clothes that show a picture of a washing machine with an X over it. It is easy to correctly guess the meaning of pictograms such as these without knowing the language of the person who wrote them. Pictograms are the most ancient form of writing.

American Indians used pictograms as a way to help people remember their oral, or spoken, history and traditions that were passed on as stories from generation to generation. The pictograms served as notes that kept the stories accurate and complete. The best-preserved examples of American Indian pictograms are the drawings they carved onto the flat surfaces of rocks. These rock drawings are called petroglyphs. (*Petro* means rock and a *glyph* is a drawing.) They have been found throughout the Americas.

The oldest American Indian petroglyphs were made in about 9000 B.C. Ancient Indians carved symbols of animals and hunting scenes into rocks. Often they carved symbols such as circles, spirals, and other geometric figures as well. These symbols did not stand for words, but they had meaning to the ancient people who made them. Modern archaeologists can only guess at what these petroglyphs mean.

Indians throughout the Americas carved or chipped petroglyphs onto rocks. These petroglyphs were found near Camp Verde, Arizona. Petroglyphs in this area were made by hitting a stone chisel with a hammer stone. They were made between A.D. 1150 and A.D. 1400. *(Library of Congress, Prints and Photographs Division [LC-USZ62-113247])*

The Chippewa (Anishinabe) of the Great Lakes region used a pointed stylus, or stick, that they made from bone or stone to draw pictograms on birch-bark scrolls. These pictograms recorded healing ceremonies that members of the Midewewin (Medicine Society) needed to know. The information on the scrolls included songs and knowledge about plants that could be used as medicine. The Chippewa also kept tallies on birch bark as well as their family histories.

Indians of the Great Plains painted pictograms that told the story of their history on buffalo hides. These records were called winter counts because each winter marked one year that had passed. The events they portrayed included good and poor hunting years, arguments with people inside and outside of the tribe, and the death of leaders. They also recorded unusual natural events. When the hides wore out, Plains Indians copied the pictograms onto new hides.

In addition to using pictograms, many American Indians who lived in Mesoamerica wrote using a system of ideographs. An

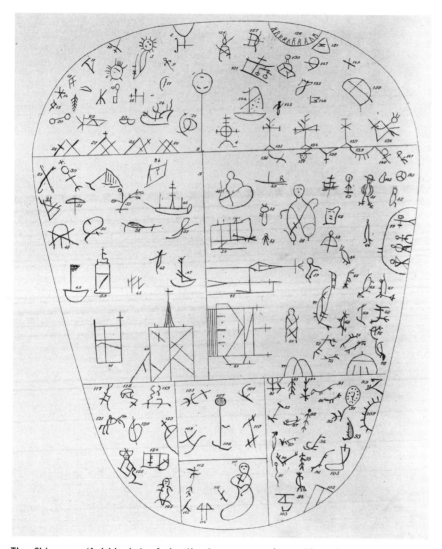

The Chippewa (Anishinabe) of the Northeast wrote by making pictures on rock and birch bark. Many of the pictures show the history of the tribe. Others recorded treatments for illnesses. Still others recorded how ceremonies were to be held. The numbers that appear on this old copy of Chippewa writing were added by Henry Rowe Schoolcraft, who published these copies he had made of Chippewa writing in a book in 1845. *(Library of Congress, Prints and Photographs Division [LC-USZ62-113247])*

▲▼▲▼▲▼▲▼▲▼▲▼▲▼▲▼▲▼▲▼▲▼▲▼▲▼▲

A NEW DISCOVERY

In 2002 a team of archaeologists found clues that the Olmec may have begun inventing writing earlier than 500 B.C. The archaeologists found pictograms on a stone roller at La Venta, the ruins of an Olmec city. They think that the Olmec spread paint or ink on the roller, which was about the size of a fist. Then the Olmec used it to print the pictograms on cloth or on people's bodies. The scientists believe that the roller could have been made in about 600 B.C. Before the roller was found, the earliest example of Olmec writing was found on a stone pillar dated about 31 B.C.

▼▲▼▲▼▲▼▲▼▲▼▲▼▲▼▲▼▲▼▲▼▲▼▲▼▲▼

ideograph is a standard symbol that represents an entire word in a certain language. An example of an ideograph that is used in the English language today is the sign &, which stands for the word *and*. To understand an ideograph, a reader needs to know what word the symbol represents and what the word means in the language spoken by the writer. Although Mesoamerican written languages were different from one another, they shared common patterns.

Many archaeologists believe that the earliest writing in Mesoamerica was that of the Zapotec, whose culture arose in the area that is now Oaxaca, Mexico, in about 500 B.C. The Zapotec used writing to record history and to express the status of rulers. The Maya also began using standard symbols in their artwork at about the same time. Later these symbols became part of the Maya writing system.

The Maya used pictograms and ideographs in their writing. They also used many symbols that represented the sounds of syllables that made up words in their spoken language. Symbols that stand for syllables are called *phonoglyphs*. Phonoglyph means "sound writing." In order to understand ideographs and phonoglyphs a reader needs to know the system of written symbols that are used and the language in which they are written. Modern linguists (scientists who study language) have identified Maya glyphs that represent parts of speech such as nouns and verbs. They have also found Maya glyphs that represent prefixes or suffixes. A prefix is attached to the beginning of a word. A suffix is attached to the end of a word. By using ideographs and phonoglyphs, the Maya could record anything spoken in their language.

Mesoamerican Indians wrote on cloth and deerskin. They also wrote on paper. The Maya and Aztec made paper from the inner bark of the wild fig tree. The Aztec called this paper *amate*, which was also their name for the fig tree. The Maya and Aztec founded papermaking towns in the areas where many of the trees grew. Different towns manufactured different types of paper. These included sheets of white paper and rolls of yellow paper.

To make paper, workers first stripped bark from the trees with stone knives. They boiled the bark so that the fibers would soften and separate. Then they arranged the fibers on a wooden drying board and pounded them with a beater. The beater was a grooved stone that was attached to a handle. Beating the bark fibers softened them and fused them together into sheets.

When the sheets of paper had dried, Mesoamerican papermakers trimmed them. Then they polished them with a heated stone to close the pores and polish the surface. Finally, papermakers applied a coating of white lime (calcium carbonate) to both sides of the sheets of paper. The lime kept ink from soaking through the paper when people wrote on it.

The Toltec, Mixtec, Maya, and Aztec collected their writings into books that they made by folding long sheets of paper like an accordion or a screen. The Toltec made the earliest Mesoamerican books. They wrote a religious encyclopedia as early as A.D. 660. Like

▲▼▲▼▲▼▲▼▲▼▲▼▲▼▲▼▲▼▲▼▲▼▲▼▲▼▲

PAPERWORK

Every year Aztec papermakers sent about 500,000 sheets of paper to the emperor in Tenochtitlán, the Aztec capital city. This was how they paid their taxes. Government tax collectors used the paper to keep records of all the taxes that they collected throughout the empire. Aztec lawyers used paper to write down what happened in courtrooms. Families used paper for documents describing the land they owned. They also wrote their family histories on paper.

▼▲▼▲▼▲▼▲▼▲▼▲▼▲▼▲▼▲▼▲▼▲▼▲▼▲▼

birch-bark scrolls and winter counts that were painted on hides, Toltec and Mixtec books were memory aids that helped people remember spoken history. The authors relied on pictograms to

Unlike the picture writing of American Indians further to the north, Mesoamerican writing used glyphs, or symbols, to stand for words, rather than things. Some glyphs represented sounds. (*Library of Congress, Prints and Photographs Division [LC-USZ62-33958]*)

record history and write how religious rituals were supposed to be held.

Early Maya books contained the histories of cities along with

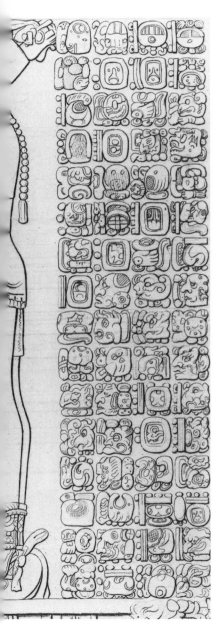

lists of the people who ruled them. The books traced the family trees of important people. They listed deaths of important people and gave descriptions of wars. Some of the books that the Maya wrote were account books that listed things that people owned, such as jewelry.

Later the Maya wrote books on astronomy and religion. These books, which were called almanacs, contained information about when certain planets would rise. Mesoamerican almanacs were made up of 260-day cycles called "day counts." Each of the days was assigned a meaning based on a cycle of 20 day names and 13 numbers. The almanacs were used to name children based on their birth dates, to set the dates of rituals, and to determine which days might be lucky or unlucky for certain activities.

The Aztec wrote almanacs as well. They also wrote history books that contained lists of years along with important events that happened in each of those years. Some books contained lists of the tributes, or taxes, that people paid to the Aztec ruler. Other books contained land records.

The Aztec called the scribes who made the books *tlacuilo*. In addition to writing, the scribes had to grind mineral pigments to make their inks. They also made inks from plants. Scribes first outlined the glyphs they were writing. Then they filled in the colors. Maya scribes used red and black ink when they made books. The main colors that Aztec scribes used were blue, red, yellow, and green. The scribes finished the books by gluing the ends of the folded paper strip to thin pieces of wood for covers. They decorated the covers of special books with paintings or with beads made of turquoise.

Aztec scribes specialized in creating one kind of book. Some worked on almanacs. Other scribes created books of family histories and land holdings. Yet others made maps. Other specialties were law books, religious books, and science books. Being a scribe was a career that was passed from parent to child. In the Aztec world, both women and men could be scribes.

Soon after conquest, Spanish missionaries encouraged Aztec and Maya scribes to make more books. They wanted to learn everything they could about the Aztec people so that they could convert them to the Catholic religion. Some of the books that they copied were copies of original books that were written hundreds of years before. The scribes continued until a royal decree from the king of Spain ordered that all American Indian books be destroyed. The 1577 decree also ordered that all books about American Indians that had been written by conquistadores and missionaries should also be burned.

American Indians developed other ways besides writing to record and share information. The Algonquian-speaking tribes of the North American Northeast wove shell beads called wampum into belts. They wove the shells, which were white and purple,

▲▼▲▼▲▼▲▼▲▼▲▼▲▼▲▼▲▼▲▼▲▼▲▼▲▼▲▼▲▼

LIBRARIES

The Aztec gathered their books into libraries. The huge library at Texcoco, a town near Tenochtitlán, the Aztec capital, served as the national archives for the Aztec. Bernal Díaz del Castillo, a priest who accompanied Cortés in Mexico, reported that Montezuma, the Aztec emperor, had a "great house full of books" before the Aztec Empire fell in 1521. Díaz del Castillo wrote: "Then we came on some towns and found idol houses and many paper books doubled together in folds like Spanish cloth, that I do not know how to describe it, seeing things as we did that had never been heard or seen before or even dreamed about." Hernán Cortés sent two books to Spain along with the first gold that the conquistadores collected from Mesoamerica.

▼▲▼▲▼▲▼▲▼▲▼▲▼▲▼▲▼▲▼▲▼▲▼▲▼▲▼▲▼

▲▼▲▼▲▼▲▼▲▼▲▼▲▼▲▼▲▼▲▼▲▼▲▼▲▼▲

A UNIVERSAL LANGUAGE

American Indians who lived on the Great Plains developed a system of hand signs to talk with others who did not speak their language. Some people of the Plateau and Great Basin also used it. American Indians invented sign language so that they could trade with other tribes. They also used it in order to "talk" silently during hunting or raiding parties when silence was critical. Plains sign language had more than 1,000 different gestures to communicate words and ideas. Plains culture groups that are known to have used sign language include the Arapaho, Cheyenne, Pawnee, Kiowa, Crow, Osage, Comanche, Pawnee, and the Dakota, Lakota, and Nakota. The Blackfeet and the Assiniboine used sign language, as did the Nez Perce and the Ute.

▼▲▼▲▼▲▼▲▼▲▼▲▼▲▼▲▼▲▼▲▼▲▼▲▼▲▼

into patterns that had meaning. They used wampum belts to record messages that runners carried from village to village. If the news was solemn or sorrowful, most of the beads on the belt were purple.

Wampum belts also were a way to record agreements. The constitution of the Iroquois League (sometimes called the Iroquois Confederacy) was recorded on a series of wampum belts. This confederacy was a formal alliance between the tribes of the Iroquois: the Oneida, Onondaga, Mohawk, Cayuga, and the Seneca. It was established between A.D. 1000 and A.D. 1400. (Later the Tuscarora joined the confederacy.) The upper half of the belt contains white shells that stood for women and the lower half contains dark shells that stood for men. One of the meanings of this wampum belt is that women and men made equal contributions to the Iroquois League.

The Inca of South America may have used the quipu, a system of knotted strings, to store information as well as numbers. Shortly after conquest, Spaniards reported that the Inca recorded poetry as well as history and religious information on their quipus. Spanish Catholic priests ordered that Inca quipus be burned to separate the Inca people from their religion and culture.

▽▲▽▲▽▲▽▲▽▲▽▲▽▲▽▲▽▲▽▲▽▲▽▲▽▲▽▲▽▲▽▲▽▲▽▲▽▲▽

A LANGUAGE FIRST

Sequoyah, a Cherokee, is the only person in the world to invent a complete written language entirely on his own. Also called George Gist, he was born in 1776 near Taskigi (Tuskeegee), Tennessee. When he grew up he made his living as a silversmith.

In 1809 a man who bought one of his pieces told him that he should sign his works. Sequoyah asked a neighbor to show him how to write his name. After seeing his name written in English, Sequoyah began thinking about creating a set of symbols that would allow people to write and read the Cherokee language.

When he first began his work, he tried using pictograms to stand for words. Soon he found that would require people to remember too many symbols. Next he tried drawing symbols for every sound in the language. He borrowed letters from the

English alphabet and invented some letters of his own to come up with 85

The Cherokee alphabet is the only alphabet in the world that was completely invented by one person. *(Library of Congress, Prints and Photographs Division [LC-USZ62-11482])*

▲▽

Some quipus have been found with knots arranged in much different patterns than the Inca used to record numbers. Modern archaeologists believe that information about the planets and stars

Sequoyah, who invented the Cherokee alphabet, was born in 1776 in what later would become Tennessee. Rather than face forced removal to Indian Territory (Oklahoma) with his people, in 1822 he joined a group of Cherokee who had moved to Mexico. He died there in 1843. In 1980 the U.S. Post Office issued a 19-cent stamp honoring him for his accomplishments. *(Library of Congress, Prints and Photographs Division [LC-USZ62-1292])*

As soon as he finished in 1821, the Cherokee tribe adopted it as their official alphabet. In the 1820s thousands of Cherokees learned to read in their own language. Sequoyah's invention allowed the Cherokees to publish the first American Indian newspaper, the *Cherokee Phoenix,* in 1828. The Cherokee called the written alphabet "talking leaves."

characters. Sequoyah tested his alphabet on his daughter, Ayoka, who quickly mastered writing in Cherokee. It took Sequoyah 12 years to create the Cherokee alphabet.

may have been recorded using the quipu. No one in modern times has been able to decode anything other than numbers from a quipu. The mystery of the information they contain remains to be solved.

9 Ecology

Ecology is a science that focuses on the relationship between living things and their environment, or surroundings. The combination of living and nonliving things in a particular environment is called an ecosystem. Ecologists (scientists who study ecology) observe how everything in an ecosystem is connected to everything else in an ecosystem.

Indians throughout the Americas practiced ecology for centuries before Europeans arrived. They observed how each part of the environment affected the other parts of the environment. Indian people understood that the patterns they saw in nature formed a balance and that it was important for them to keep that balance.

American Indians held certain places in the landscape to be especially sacred. Some of these places were those where American Indians believed the first people of their tribe were created. Other places were locations where sacred events in the tribe's history had taken place. American Indians conducted religious ceremonies at these sacred places over the centuries.

Even though different groups of Indian people practiced ceremonies that were unique to their people, most American Indians shared a common thread of belief. They believed that human beings were a small part of a very large family that included human beings, animals, plants, and the land itself. Because of their beliefs, many groups of Indian people valued cooperation. They believed that plants, animals, the land, wind, and water were partners. One was no better or more important than any other.

For most American Indians, everything on Earth was a potential helper or teacher. For example, American Indians did not think of wild plants as weeds as Europeans did. Instead, Indian people used

Earth served as shelter for the Mandan people who lived In thls earth lodge. The Mandan lived along what is now the Missouri River in North Dakota. The earth that covered their homes kept them warm in winter and cool in summer. This picture was taken in 1910. A bull boat, a boat made from hide, leans against the doorway. *(Edward S. Curtis Collection, Library of Congress, Prints and Photographs Division [LC-USZ62-114582])*

them as food, medicine, fiber, and dye. American Indians used the resources that the Earth provided to feed and clothe themselves and to make items they used in their daily lives. They were careful not to use up these important resources, which their lives depended on. The wise use of natural resources, such as forests, animals, and minerals in the soil, is called conservation.

Europeans who came to the Americas did not share the same beliefs as American Indians. They believed that human beings were meant to control nature for their own gain. Unlike American Indians, European colonists looked for ways to make money from their environment. The easiest way to do this was to ship lumber, animal hides, and minerals to Europe. The idea that human beings needed to conserve natural resources did begin not to take hold in North America until the mid-1800s. In 1849 the U.S. government, fearing that all of the trees on the continent would soon

American Indians found many uses for the wild plants that they gathered. They ate the first shoots of milkweed plants that came up in the spring after boiling them many times to make them safe to eat. Some tribes boiled milkweed sap and chewed it like gum. Others mixed the sap with colored pigments from the earth in order to make paint. Indian people used milkweed sap as a lotion for poison ivy rashes. They also spun milkweed fiber into yarn and used the fluff for starting fires. *(U.S. Fish and Wildlife Service)*

▲▽▲▽▲▽▲▽▲▽▲▽▲▽▲▽▲▽▲▽▲▽▲▽▲▽▲▽▲

ZOOS AND GARDENS

Aztec emperors of Mesoamerica established huge zoos. The animals that they contained included jaguars, wolves, and foxes. They were fed turkeys. Some Aztec zoos had large houses where birds were kept. The Aztec emperors also collected plants, which they displayed in botanical gardens. The zoos and gardens were for amusement and also served as places where animals and plants could be studied.

▼▲▼▲▼▲▼▲▼▲▼▲▼▲▼▲▼▲▼▲▼▲▼▲▼▲▼▲▼

be cut and sold, established the Department of the Interior to protect timber and other natural resources. The modern science of ecology developed in the mid-1900s in response to concern about air and water pollution and other human-caused damage to the environment.

CONSERVING FOOD RESOURCES

In the upper Midwest of North America, the Chippewa (Anishinabe), who harvested wild rice on the lakes of what are now Minnesota and Wisconsin, only took part of the rice. They made sure that they left enough rice to serve as seed so that the rice would continue to grow in the lakes. They used canoes when they harvested wild rice. The canoes moved between the rice plants without damaging them. To the Chippewa people, rice was a sacred plant.

In the 1960s non-Indians began harvesting wild rice in flat-bottomed boats that crushed the stems of the

▲▽▲▽▲▽▲▽▲▽▲▽▲▽▲▽▲▽▲▽▲▽▲▽▲▽▲

SALMON AND FORESTS

Modern scientists have found that salmon are important to the forests that surround the rivers in which they live. They found that plants that grew on the banks of streams and rivers where salmon spawned each year were higher in nitrogen than other plants. Nitrogen is an element that is important for plant growth. Large, healthy trees along river and stream banks provide the salmon with shade so that the water is the right temperature to keep salmon eggs alive. The branches that fall into the river provide protection for young salmon.

▼▲▼▲▼▲▼▲▼▲▼▲▼▲▼▲▼▲▼▲▼▲▼▲▼▲▼

Pacific salmon are diminishing due to commercial fishing. Indians traditionally did not try to catch all the salmon so that the fish could continue to breed. *(Timothy Knepp/U.S. Fish and Wildlife Service)*

rice plants. The non-Indian rice harvesters took all the rice that they could leaving few seeds to grow rice plants. American Indians were concerned that soon there would be no more rice. They worked to get the Minnesota legislature to pass a law that required anyone gathering rice on public land to use traditional Indian rice harvesting methods.

Indians of the Northwest who fished for salmon did not try to snare all of them from the streams where the fish came to lay their eggs each year, although they had the ability to do this. They understood that to continue harvesting fish, they had to conserve this resource. Today Pacific salmon are disappearing from the streams where they once spawned (laid eggs) in Alaska and the Northwest because of commercial fishing.

The survival of American Indians of the northern plains tribes depended on the buffalo, or bison. Indians of the Plains used every part of the animal. They ate the meat and used buffalo hides (skins) for tipi covers, blankets, and clothing. They used bison fat for skin

△▽△▽△▽△▽△▽△▽△▽△▽△▽△▽△▽△▽△▽△▽△

BUFFALO JUMPS

Until the introduction of the horse to the Great Plains in the 1700s, American Indians who lived there hunted buffalo by chasing herds of them over cliffs at sites that are called buffalo jumps today. The Indians dried the meat to preserve it for later use. Because there were such great numbers of buffalo living on the plains, this method of hunting did not threaten them with extinction. The number of animals that American Indian hunters killed was small in comparison to the number killed by non-Indian buffalo hunters with guns.

▽△▽△▽△▽△▽△▽△▽△▽△▽△▽△▽△▽△▽△▽

lotion and bison bones for sled runners and tools. Indians used bison sinew (the fiber that connects muscle to bone) for thread and for bowstrings.

Starting in the 1840s non-Indian buffalo hunters began killing bison to feed workers who built railroad tracks across the West. They also shot bison to feed U.S. Army troops. Later they began killing bison only for their hides, which they sold to people in the East and in Europe. Professional non-Indian hunters killed between 100 and 300 animals a day for their hides. They skinned the animals and left their carcasses to rot. By 1887, fewer than 1,000 bison were left on the Great Plains. Today, through the efforts of conservationists and American Indian tribes, the number of bison has grown to about 500,000.

△▽△▽△▽△▽△▽△▽△▽△▽△▽△▽△▽△▽△▽△▽△

A HUMAN-MADE ECOSYSTEM

Mesoamerican Indian farmers grew their crops on *chinampas,* raised beds of soil surrounded by canals. This method of farming created an ecosystem. When soil was washed into the canals by rain, it provided nutrients for water plants that grew in the canals. Farmers of Mesoamerica harvested these plants and piled them on their fields to enrich the soil. The *chinampas* attracted birds, and the canals were filled with fish. The fish and birds were another source of food. The Spanish conquistadores did not understand this system of farming and failed to maintain the garden plots and the canals. Today the canals are filled with treated sewage and industrial waste.

▽△▽△▽△▽△▽△▽△▽△▽△▽△▽△▽△▽△▽△▽△▽

By observing nature, American Indian farmers learned how to deliberately plant and harvest plants. They domesticated (tamed) many food plants including, corn, beans, squash, peppers, tomatoes, potatoes, and pineapples. This picture of a pineapple was drawn by an early Spanish visitor to the Caribbean. *(Library of Congress, Prints and Photographs Division [LC-USZC4-5349])*

American Indian farmers of North America cleared trees from thousands of acres of the land so that they could grow crops such as corn, beans, and squash. A typical clearing in what is now Ontario, Canada, ranged from between 150 and 600 acres. After growing crops on cleared fields for several years, Indian farmers abandoned those fields and cleared new ones. This allowed the land to rest. After about 20 years, wild plants and trees reestablished themselves so that the fields became forest once more.

The forest was as important to the Indian people of the Northeast and Southeast as their fields were. The forest gave them wood and bark for making their homes. It also gave them firewood for heating their homes. Indian people of the Northeast used tree roots for fiber to sew together birch-bark panels when they made their canoes. Indian people of the Southeast used large tree trunks to make dugout canoes. The forests were home to the game animals and birds that many American Indians hunted for food. The forests also provided Indian people with plants that they used as medicines.

European colonists took over American Indian fields after driving the people from them. Then they began clearing more land to make the fields bigger. As new colonists arrived from Europe, they cleared even more land. Soon there were very few trees in some areas of the Northeast.

The forests that had trapped and held water after rainstorms so that it would slowly drain into streams were gone. When the trees were gone, rainwater evaporated more quickly than before. (Evaporation is when water becomes vapor and is carried off by the air.) Many streams dried up. The rivers that the streams had fed became smaller. Heavy rains washed soil from the bare land once covered by trees into other streams and muddied the waters of the rivers.

As colonists cleared the forests, game animals and birds no longer could live on the land that they had cleared. American Indians were unable to feed their people by hunting. American Indian leaders of the Northeast tried to explain to the settlers how their actions were destroying the environment. When the colonists did not listen to them and continued cutting trees, wars broke out between the Indians and the North American colonists.

CONSERVING WATER

American Indians who did not live in areas where water was plentiful found ways to conserve it. Ancient farmers of the Americas invented irrigation methods that cut down on the amount of water lost through evaporation. To save water, the Anasazi, whose culture began to flourish in the North American desert Southwest in about 350 B.C., built thousands of acres of terraces that trapped water from rainstorms so that it would sink into the soil where they planted crops. Extra water ran down to the next terrace to water another garden plot. Ancient farmers living in the Andes of South America used a similar method of terracing that conserved water.

In what are now Arizona and Utah, Anasazi farmers placed rocks in lines to form borders on sloping land. This slowed the water runoff and held the soil in place. Anasazi farmers arranged oblong, flat stones in rows around their crops in order to prevent wind damage as well.

Anasazi water engineers made irrigation ditches that they lined with stones. These ditches carried rainwater to crops. The stones prevented water from seeping into the dry soil along the way to the fields. The Hohokam, who began living in what is now Arizona in about 300 B.C., lined their irrigation ditches with clay and limestone.

The Anasazi people who lived in Canyon de Chelly, in what is now Arizona, built their homes in natural shelters in the canyon wall. They farmed on the floor of the canyon where their crops would receive water runoff after rainstorms. This picture was taken in 1873. These abandoned homes still stand today. *(Library of Congress, Prints and Photographs Division [LC-USZ62-3874])*

The Maya of Mesoamerica used the position of stars and planets to locate their cities. Often these cities were far from sources of drinking water. The Maya built their cities around large plazas and finished them with a type of concrete called *sacbe*. When they built these plazas, they made certain that they tilted slightly. As it rained, water drained from the plazas into limestone cisterns that they had built. A cistern is an underground tank that is used for storing water. The Maya built some of their homes with roofs that were slanted too. Rainwater drained into cisterns so that the people who lived in these houses had drinking water.

MANAGING FORESTS

American Indians had been deliberately shaping the forests for thousands of years before Europeans arrived in the Americas. Because they used brush for fuel, they cleared the forests of dead wood and undergrowth near their villages. This helped to lower the risk of uncontrolled forest fires started by lightning.

American Indians also used fire as a tool to lower the danger of wildfires. About every two to three years, they set fires to rid the forests of underbrush. They planned these fires and knew how to use backfires to control larger fires. A backfire is a controlled burn that destroys fuel that the fire needs to keep burning so that the fire will burn itself out. American Indians taught settlers on the Plains how to use backfires to protect their cabins and wagons during prairie wildfires.

Controlled burns were helpful in many ways. These fires rid the forest of small trees that competed with larger pines and hardwoods. American Indians used these larger trees for making their canoes and for building their homes. The large trees were able to grow larger. Controlled fires also encouraged new growth of plants, such as ferns, on the forest floor. This attracted deer and other animals that ate these young plants. Modern forest management research has shown that deer that eat new growth after a fire produce more and healthier offspring than those that eat older plants. Controlled burns also provided more food for Indian people. They added nutrients to the soil that increased new growth on wild blackberry, blueberry, and huckleberry bushes. They also caused the bushes to produce more berries.

The fires that the North American Indians set created parklike grassy areas. These clearings attracted game that the Indians

The American Indian firefighters in this picture dug a firebreak (a space free of anything that could burn) in order to stop a forest fire from spreading in Arkansas. This picture was taken in 1956. Today teams of American Indians continue to work for the Forest Service, the Bureau of Land Management, and other agencies as firefighters. *(Photograph No. 95-G-466941 National Forest Service Collection, National Archives and Records Administration—College Park)*

hunted. They also made hunting easier for the Indians. It was easier to travel through forests that did not have thick underbrush. It was also easier for the American Indian hunters to see the animals they were hunting. Removing the underbrush provided American Indians safety from bands of enemies who might try to catch them unaware.

Sometimes American Indians set fires to control pests. Indians who lived along the Gulf Coast and those who lived in what is now Alaska used the burns to cut down the number of insects that bred in dense underbrush. The explorer Álvar Núñez Cabeza de Vaca noted that during the 1530s American Indians in Texas set fire to underbrush to drive off mosquitoes. American Indians of the Southeast used controlled burns to drive poisonous snakes from the

American Indians used fire to thin the forests of brush and small trees. This allowed the big trees to grow even larger. A U.S. Fish and Wildlife worker stands in front of an old-growth tree in this photograph to show its size. *(John and Karen Hollingsworth/U.S. Fish and Wildlife Service)*

woods. Because so little underbrush remained, travelers could more easily see the snakes that had stayed.

On the prairies, where there were few trees, American Indians set fire to the tall grass that grew there. This encouraged new grass to grow. They also used fires to drive buffalo to cliffs. When the buffalo jumped over the cliffs, Indian people, who had set up camp at the bottom of the cliffs, would butcher the animals.

In areas such as the Missouri and Mississippi river basins, carefully planned forest fires created more grazing area for the buffalo. This meant that the buffalo moved closer to Indian settlements, so that hunting was easier. Controlled burning expanded the range of the buffalo so that by A.D. 1000, buffalo lived east of the Mississippi. This provided a new source of food for Indians of the Northeast.

European colonists did not understand the importance of controlled burns. Once they had removed the Indians from the land, they failed to clear the forests of underbrush. The forests that they did not clear for farming grew wild until they became fire hazards. In some areas non-Indian lumberjacks harvested most of the trees, leaving the limbs and stumps behind. This created even more of a fire hazard. By the late 1800s huge forest fires called firestorms blazed across the Northeast and the Great Lakes states. After these disasters, the U.S. government set aside land for national forests and established the U.S. Forest Service to manage them.

American Indians found hunting to be much easier when they cleared open spaces in the forest. Deliberate burns created open spaces. The burns increased the number of game animals by increasing the growth of plants that these animals ate. This drawing of Indians hunting in Louisiana was made in 1758. *(Library of Congress, Prints and Photographs Division [LC-USZ62-677])*

In 1969 the U.S. Congress passed the National Environmental Policy Act, creating the Environmental Protection Agency (EPA). The mission of this agency is "to protect human health and to

By shaping the landscape with fire, American Indians provided more areas where buffalo (bison) could graze. Although herds of bison were naturally concentrated in the Great Plains, American Indians extended their range to the Northeast as well. *(U.S. Fish and Wildlife Service)*

safeguard the natural environment—air, water, and land—upon which life depends."

Modern ecologists owe a debt to American Indians. In November 1995, President Bill Clinton gave credit to the American Indian people in a proclamation that declared the month of November as American Indian Heritage Month. "The gift of wisdom is one that our society has struggled with," President Clinton said. "Living in harmony with nature instead of seeking domination, American Indians have shown us how to be responsible for our environment, to treasure the beauty and resources of the land and water for which we are stewards, and to preserve them for the generations who will come after us."

GLOSSARY OF ANCIENT CULTURES OF THE AMERICAS

This glossary lists some of the important cultures, empires, and city-states in the Americas before 1492. Many of them existed hundreds or thousands of years before Europeans arrived in the Americas. Archaeologists try to piece together the history of America's ancient people from their buildings and the smaller objects they left behind. They can only make educated guesses based on the artifacts that they find.

The history of ancient America is one of changes. Because of this, modern people often mistakenly think that entire groups of ancient Indian people disappeared. Indian people and their civilizations did not vanish. Governments rose to power, fell, and were replaced by other governments. Sometimes large groups of people moved. They shared ideas with their neighbors and borrowed ideas from them. The Indians who made up civilizations of the past are the ancestors of the Indians of the Americas who are alive today.

Adena   The Adena culture arose along the valleys of the Mississippi and Ohio Rivers and lasted from about 1500 B.C. to A.D. 200. Adena people were farmers and built burial mounds. The Hopewell people followed them.

Anasazi   The Anasazi lived in the southwestern part of what is now the United States in New Mexico, Arizona, Utah, and Colorado. Their culture flourished from about 350 B.C. to

A.D. 1450. They are thought to be the ancestors of modern Pueblo people.

Aztec (Mexica) The Aztec moved into the Valley of Mexico from the north in about A.D. 1100. Their culture followed that of the Toltec in the region. By 1350 they had expanded their empire and became the dominant state in what became central Mexico. They were the powerful group in that area when the Spaniards arrived. At its largest, the main Aztec city of Tenochtitlán had about 250,000 residents.

Chalchihuite The Chalchihuite people entered what is now the Sierra Madre of Mexico between A.D. 900 and 1250. They were colonized by the Aztec after the Aztec Empire rose to power. They lived in what was considered the northern frontier of the Aztec Empire.

Chavin Chavin culture flourished in the fertile river valleys of what is now Peru from about 1000 B.C. to about 200 B.C. The Chavin lived about 1,200 to 2,000 years before the Inca Empire was established.

Chimu The Chimu civilization lasted from 1100 A.D. to the mid-1400s in what is now Peru. The Chimu state was conquered by the Inca.

Chinchorro The Chinchorro culture, on the coast of what is now Peru, began in about 5000 B.C. It reached its peak in about 3000 B.C. The Chinchorro are best known for the elaborate ways in which they mummified their dead. They are one of the most ancient cultures to have lived in the region.

Hohokam The Hohokam culture arose in what is now central and southern Arizona in about 300 B.C. Hohokam people are thought to be the ancestors of the Akimel O'odham (Pima) and the Tohono O'odham (Papago). The Hohokam lived in the Southwest in the same time period as the Anasazi. Their settlements were south of those of the Anasazi.

Hopewell Hopewell culture arose along the valleys of the Mississippi and Ohio Rivers in about 300 B.C. The Hopewell are considered part of the Mound Builders, along with the Adena people who came before them. They built huge earthworks and flourished until about A.D. 700. They were followed by the Mississippian Culture.

Inca   The Inca established an empire in what is now Peru in about A.D. 1000 and rapidly expanded it. This empire extended from what is now northwest Argentina to parts of what is now Colombia. The Inca Empire was in power when the Spanish conquistador Francisco Pizarro arrived in South America.

Iroquois League (Haudenosaunee)   The Iroquois League, or Haudenosaunee, was an alliance of Northeast tribes established some time between A.D. 1000 and 1400. The tribes included the Oneida, Mohawk, Cayuga, Onondaga, Seneca, and later the Tuscarora.

Maya   The Maya civilization arose in what is now the Yucatán Peninsula of Mexico starting in about 1500 B.C. They did not have a centralized government but instead formed city-states. Maya people also lived in what are now Belize, Guatemala, El Salvador, and Honduras. When the Aztec expanded their empire, they began collecting taxes from the Maya and demanded loyalty to the Aztec Emperor.

Mississippian Culture   The Mississippian Culture arose in about A.D. 1000. Sometimes these people are called temple mound builders. Unlike the Adena and Hopewell people, they built earthworks for temples and ceremonial centers, rather than for burials. They built Cahokia, a city of about 30,000 people, near what is St. Louis, Missouri, today. Mississippian Culture started to weaken in the 1500s, but early French explorers encountered some temple mound builders in the late 1600s.

Mixtec   The Mixtec lived in what is now southern Mexico. Their culture arose in about A.D. 900. The Aztec Empire eventually dominated the Mixtec city-states, but their culture continued to thrive until the arrival of the Spaniards.

Moche   The Moche culture arose on the northern coast of what is now Peru in about 200 B.C. It flourished until about A.D. 600. The Moche were master artists.

Mound Builders   These were American Indians of several cultures who lived in the Mississippi and Ohio River Valleys over a period of time. Some Mound Builders also lived in the Southeast. These people of the Adena, Hopewell, and Mississippian cultures built extensive earthworks.

Nazca   The Nazca people lived in the lowlands of what is now Peru. Their culture arose starting in about 600 B.C. and lasted until about A.D. 900. Later the area where they lived became part of the Inca Empire.

Old Copper Culture Peoples who lived from about 4000 B.C. to 1500 B.C. in the Great Lakes region of North America. These Indians worked with copper deposits that were close to the surface of the Earth. They made some of the earliest metal tools and objects in the world.

Olmec The Olmec culture flourished starting in about 1700 B.C. in the coastal lowlands of what is now Mexico. It lasted until about 400 B.C. The Olmec built several cities, including La Venta, which had a population of about 18,000. The Olmec are also known as the Rubber People because they made items from rubber.

Paracas The Paracas culture arose in the river valleys of what is now Peru in about 1300 B.C. and flourished until about A.D. 20. Paracas people invented many weaving and pottery techniques. A thousand years later, the area where they lived became part of the Inca Empire.

Paleo-Indians A general term for those who lived before about 4000 B.C. They were the oldest peoples of the Americas. They hunted for their food, killing large mammals, such as the wooly mammoth and the mastodon.

Poverty Point Culture The people of Poverty Point lived in the Lower Mississippi Valley between 1730 and 1350 B.C. They are a small, distinct group within Mississippian, or Mound Building, Culture.

Teotihuacán The Teotihuacán culture flourished in the central valley of what is now Mexico from about 1000 B.C. to 900 A.D. At its center was the city-state of Teotihuacán, which was at its strongest from about A.D. 1 to about 650. In A.D. 500 the city was home to between 100,000 and 200,000 people.

Thule The Thule culture arose in what is now northwestern Alaska between 1,000 and 2,000 years ago. Then it spread to Greenland. Thule people were the ancestors of the Inuit. They are known for their tool-making ability.

Toltec The Toltec migrated into what is now known as the Valley of Mexico in central Mexico in about A.D. 800. They established their capital at Tula in about 900. About 60,000 people lived in Tula. The Toltec rule lasted until some time in the

1100s, when invading groups attacked and overthrew them. Little is known about the Toltec because the Aztec used the ruins of Tula as a source of building materials for their own monuments.

Zapotec   The Zapotec established a city-state south of the Mixtec in what is now southern Mexico. In about 500 B.C. they began building the city of Monte Albán. By A.D. 450, more than 15,000 people lived in Monte Albán. Later this grew to 25,000 people. By about 700 A.D. the Zapotec began moving away from their city. Although their culture remained, the Zapotec no longer had a city-state.

TRIBES ORGANIZED BY CULTURE AREA

North American Culture Areas

ARCTIC CULTURE AREA
Aleut
Inuit

CALIFORNIA CULTURE AREA
Achomawi (Pit River)
Akwaala
Alliklik (Tataviam)
Atsugewi (Pit River)
Bear River
Cahto (Kato)
Cahuilla
Chilula
Chimariko
Chumash
Costanoan (Ohlone)
Cupeño
Diegueño (Ipai)
Esselen
Fernandeño
Gabrieliño
Huchnom
Hupa
Ipai (Diegueño)
Juaneño
Kamia (Tipai)
Karok
Kitanemuk

Konomihu
Lassik
Luiseño
Maidu
Mattole
Miwok
Nicoleño
Nomlaki
Nongatl
Okwanuchu
Patwin (subgroup of Wintun)
Pomo
Salinas
Serrano
Shasta
Sinkyone
Tolowa (Smith River)
Tubatulabal (Kern River)
Vanyume
Wailaki
Wappo
Whilkut
Wintu (subgroup of Wintun)
Wintun
Wiyot
Yahi

Yana
Yokuts
Yuki
Yurok

GREAT BASIN CULTURE AREA
Bannock
Chemehuevi
Kawaiisu
Mono
Paiute
Panamint
Sheepeater (subgroup
of Bannock
and Shoshone)
Shoshone
Snake (subgroup of Paiute)
Ute
Washoe

GREAT PLAINS CULTURE AREA
Arapaho
Arikara
Assiniboine
Atsina (Gros Ventre)
Blackfeet
Blood (subgroup of Blackfeet)
Cheyenne
Comanche
Crow
Hidatsa
Ioway
Kaw
Kichai
Kiowa
Kiowa-Apache
Mandan
Missouria
Omaha
Osage
Otoe
Pawnee
Piegan (subgroup of Blackfeet)

Plains Cree
Plains Ojibway
Ponca
Quapaw
Sarcee
Sioux (Dakota, Lakota, Nakota)
Tawakoni
Tawehash
Tonkawa
Waco
Wichita
Yscani

NORTHEAST CULTURE AREA
Abenaki
Algonkin
Amikwa (Otter)
Cayuga
Chippewa (Ojibway,
Anishinabe)
Chowanoc
Conoy
Coree (Coranine)
Erie
Fox (Mesquaki)
Hatteras
Honniasont
Huron (Wyandot)
Illinois
Iroquois (Haudenosaunee)
Kickapoo
Kitchigami
Lenni Lenape (Delaware)
Machapunga
Mahican
Maliseet
Manhattan (subgroup of Lenni
Lenape or Wappinger)
Massachuset
Mattabesac
Meherrin
Menominee
Miami

Micmac

Mingo (subgroup of Iroquois)

Mohawk

Mohegan

Montauk

Moratok

Nanticoke

Narragansett

Nauset

Neusiok

Neutral (Attiwandaronk)

Niantic

Nipmuc

Noquet

Nottaway

Oneida

Onondaga

Ottawa

Otter (Amikwa)

Pamlico (Pomeiok)

Passamaquoddy

Paugussett

Penacook

Penobscot

Pequot

Pocomtuc

Poospatuck
(subgroup of Montauk)

Potawatomi

Powhatan

Raritan
(subgroup of Lenni Lenape)

Roanoke

Sac

Sakonnet

Secotan

Seneca

Shawnee

Shinnecock
(subgroup of Montauk)

Susquehannock

Tobacco (Petun)

Tuscarora

Wampanoag

Wappinger

Weapemeoc

Wenro

Winnebago (Ho-Chunk)

**NORTHWEST COAST
CULTURE AREA**

Ahantchuyuk

Alsea

Atfalati

Bella Coola

Cathlamet

Cathlapotle

Chastacosta

Chehalis

Chelamela

Chepenafa (Mary's River)

Chetco

Chilluckittequaw

Chimakum

Chinook

Clackamas

Clallam

Clatskanie

Clatsop

Clowwewalla

Comox

Coos

Coquille (Mishikhwutmetunne)

Cowichan

Cowlitz

Dakubetede

Duwamish

Gitskan

Haida

Haisla

Heiltsuk

Kalapuya

Kuitsh

Kwakiutl

Kwalhioqua
Latgawa
Luckiamute
Lumni
Makah
Miluk
Muckleshoot
Multomah (Wappato)
Nanaimo
Nisga
Nisqually
Nooksack
Nootka
Puntlatch
Puyallup
Quaitso (Queets)
Quileute
Quinault
Rogue
Sahehwamish
Samish
Santiam
Seechelt
Semiahmoo
Siletz
Siuslaw
Skagit
Skilloot
Skykomish
Snohomish
Snoqualmie
Songish
Squamish
Squaxon (Squaxin)
Stalo
Swallah
Swinomish
Takelma (Rogue)
Taltushtuntude
Tillamook
Tlingit
Tsimshian

Tututni (Rogue)
Twana
Umpqua
Wappato (Multomah)
Wasco
Watlala (Cascade)
Yamel
Yaquina
Yoncalla

PLATEAU CULTURE AREA
Cayuse
Chelan
Coeur d'Alene
Columbia (Sinkiuse)
Colville
Entiat
Flathead (Salish)
Kalispel
Klamath
Klickitat
Kootenai (Flathead)
Lake (Senijextee)
Lillooet
Methow
Modoc
Molalla
Nez Perce
Ntlakyapamuk (Thompson)
Okanagan
Palouse
Pshwanwapam
Sanpoil
Shuswap
Sinkaietk
Sinkakaius
Skin (Tapanash)
Spokan
Stuwihamuk
Taidnapam
Tenino
Tyigh

Umatilla
Walla Walla
Wanapam
Wauyukma
Wenatchee
Wishram
Yakama

SOUTHEAST CULTURE AREA
Acolapissa
Adai
Ais
Akokisa
Alabama
Amacano
Apalachee
Apalachicola
Atakapa
Avoyel
Bayogoula
Bidai
Biloxi
Caddo
Calusa
Caparaz
Cape Fear
Catawba
Chakchiuma
Chatot
Chawasha (subgroup
of Chitimacha)
Cheraw (Sara)
Cherokee
Chiaha
Chickasaw
Chine
Chitimacha
Choctaw
Congaree
Coushatta
Creek
Cusabo
Deadose

Eno
Eyeish (Ayish)
Griga
Guacata
Guale
Hitchiti
Houma
Ibitoupa
Jeaga
Kaskinampo
Keyauwee
Koroa
Lumbee
Manahoac
Miccosukee
(subgroup of Seminole)
Mobile
Monacan
Moneton
Muklasa
Nahyssan
Napochi
Natchez
Occaneechi
Oconee
Ofo
Okelousa
Okmulgee
Opelousa
Osochi
Pasacagoula
Patiri
Pawokti
Pee Dee
Pensacola
Quinipissa
Santee (Issati)
Saponi
Sawokli
Seminole
Sewee
Shakori
Sissipahaw

Sugeree
Taensa
Tamathli
Tangipahoa
Taposa
Tawasa
Tekesta
Timucua
Tiou
Tohome
Tunica
Tuskegee
Tutelo
Waccamaw
Washa (subgroup of
Chitimacha)
Wateree
Waxhaw
Winyaw
Woccon
Yadkin
Yamasee
Yazoo
Yuchi

SOUTHWEST CULTURE AREA
Akimel O'odham (Pima)
Apache
Coahuiltec
Cocopah
Halchidhoma
Halyikwamai
Havasupai
Hopi
Hualapai
Jumano (Shuman)
Karankawa
Keres (Pueblo Indians)
Kohuana
Maricopa
Mojave
Navajo (Dineh)
Piro (Pueblo Indians)

Pueblo
Quenchan (Yuma)
Shuman (Jumano)
Sobaipuri
Tewa (Pueblo Indians)
Tiwa (Pueblo Indians)
Tohono O'odham (Papago)
Towa (Jemez, Pueblo Indians)
Yaqui
Yavapai
Yuma (Quechan)
Zuni

SUBARCTIC CULTURE AREA
Ahtena (Copper)
Beaver (Tsattine)
Beothuk
Carrier
Chilcotin
Chipewyan
Cree
Dogrib
Eyak
Han
Hare (Kawchottine)
Ingalik
Kolchan
Koyukon
Kutchin
Montagnais
Nabesna
Nahane
Naskapi
Sekani
Slave (Slavery,
Etchaottine)
Tahltan
Tanaina
Tanana
Tatsanottine (Yellowknife)
Tsetsaut
Tutchone (Mountain)

Mesoamerican Culture Area*

Aztec (Mexica-Nahuatl)   Olmec
Chalchiuites   Toltec
Maya   Zapotec
Mixtec

Circum-Caribbean Culture Area
(West Indies and Portion of Central America)

Arawak   Matagalpa
Boruca   Mosquito
Carib   Paya
Ciboney   Rama
Ciguayo   Silam
Coiba   Sumo
Corobici   Taino
Cuna   Talamanca
Guaymi   Ulva
Guetar   Voto
Jicaque   Yosco
Lucayo

South American Culture Areas*

ANDEAN CULTURE AREA
Achuari
Aguaruna
Chavin
Chimu
Inca
Jivaro
Mapuche
Moche
Nazca
Quecha

**CENTRAL AND
SOUTHERN CULTURE AREA**
Guarani
Mapuche

**TROPICAL FOREST (AMAZON
BASIN) CULTURE AREA**
Arawak
Carib
Tupi

* These lists do not attempt to include all groups in the area. They do, however, include a mix of ancient and modern peoples.

Appendix
MAPS

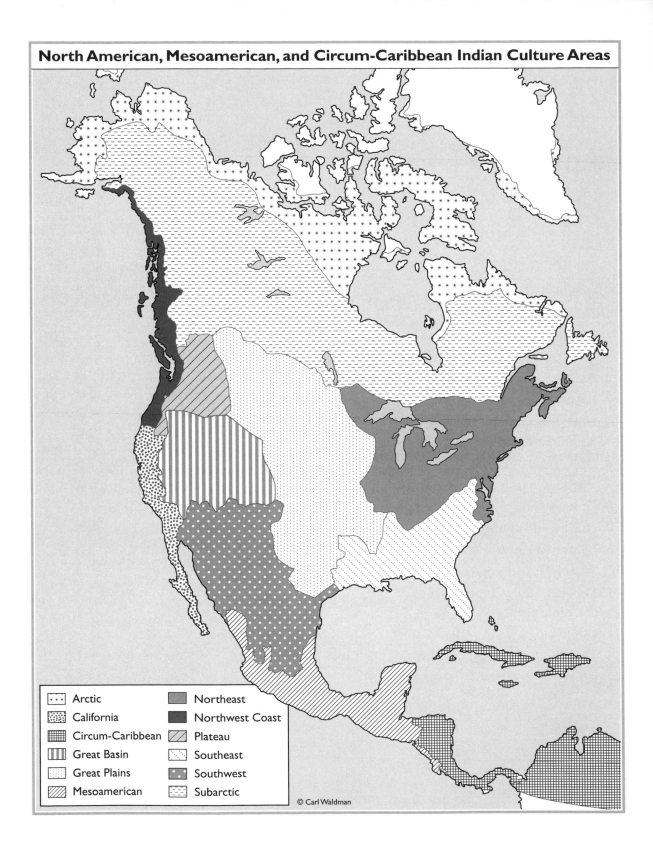

North American, Mesoamerican, and Circum-Caribbean Indian Culture Areas

Arctic
California
Circum-Caribbean
Great Basin
Great Plains
Mesoamerican
Northeast
Northwest Coast
Plateau
Southeast
Southwest
Subarctic

© Carl Waldman

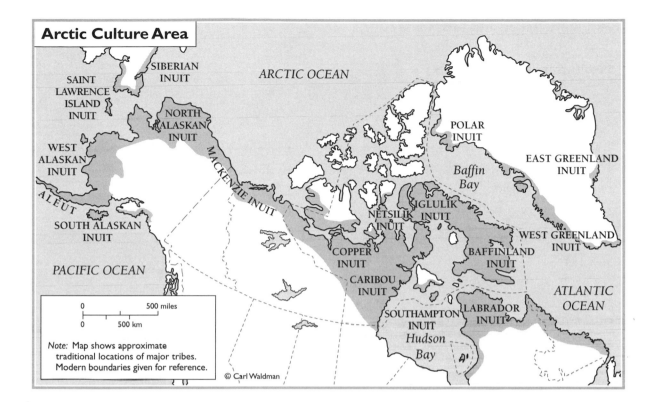

Arctic Culture Area

ARCTIC OCEAN

SAINT LAWRENCE ISLAND INUIT

SIBERIAN INUIT

NORTH ALASKAN INUIT

WEST ALASKAN INUIT

ALEUT

SOUTH ALASKAN INUIT

PACIFIC OCEAN

MACKENZIE INUIT

COPPER INUIT

NETSILIK INUIT

IGLULIK INUIT

Baffin Bay

POLAR INUIT

EAST GREENLAND INUIT

WEST GREENLAND INUIT

BAFFINLAND INUIT

CARIBOU INUIT

SOUTHAMPTON INUIT

Hudson Bay

LABRADOR INUIT

ATLANTIC OCEAN

0   500 miles
0   500 km

Note: Map shows approximate traditional locations of major tribes. Modern boundaries given for reference.

© Carl Waldman

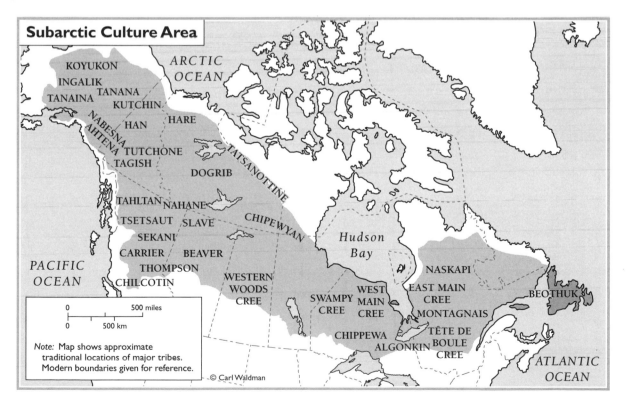

Subarctic Culture Area

ARCTIC OCEAN

KOYUKON

INGALIK

TANAINA   TANANA
          KUTCHIN

NABESNA   HAN   HARE
AHTENA

TUTCHONE
TAGISH

TATSANOTTINE

DOGRIB

TAHLTAN   NAHANE

TSETSAUT   SLAVE   CHIPEWYAN

SEKANI

CARRIER   BEAVER

THOMPSON

CHILCOTIN

WESTERN WOODS CREE

Hudson Bay

SWAMPY CREE

WEST MAIN CREE

NASKAPI

EAST MAIN CREE

MONTAGNAIS

BEOTHUK

CHIPPEWA

ALGONKIN

TÊTE DE BOULE CREE

PACIFIC OCEAN

ATLANTIC OCEAN

0   500 miles
0   500 km

Note: Map shows approximate traditional locations of major tribes. Modern boundaries given for reference.

© Carl Waldman

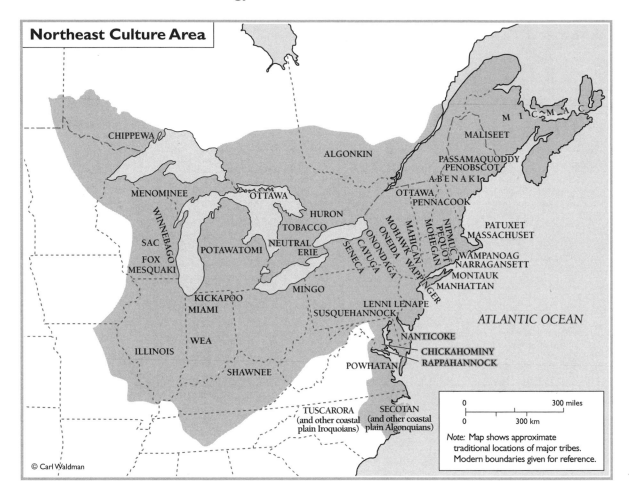

Northeast Culture Area

M I C M A C
MALISEET
CHIPPEWA
ALGONKIN
PASSAMAQUODDY
PENOBSCOT
A B E N A K I
MENOMINEE
OTTAWA
OTTAWA,
PENNACOOK
WINNEBAGO
HURON
NIPMUC
TOBACCO
PATUXET
PEQUOT
MASSACHUSET
MOHAWK
MAHICAN
MOHEGAN
SAC
NEUTRAL
ONEIDA
WAMPANOAG
POTAWATOMI
ERIE
ONONDAGA
NARRAGANSETT
FOX
CAYUGA
WAPPINGER
MONTAUK
MESQUAKI
SENECA
MANHATTAN
KICKAPOO
MINGO
LENNI LENAPE
MIAMI
SUSQUEHANNOCK
ATLANTIC OCEAN
WEA
NANTICOKE
ILLINOIS
CHICKAHOMINY
POWHATAN
RAPPAHANNOCK
SHAWNEE

0		300 miles
0	300 km	

TUSCARORA   SECOTAN
(and other coastal   (and other coastal
plain Iroquoians)   plain Algonquians)

Note: Map shows approximate
traditional locations of major tribes.
Modern boundaries given for reference.

© Carl Waldman

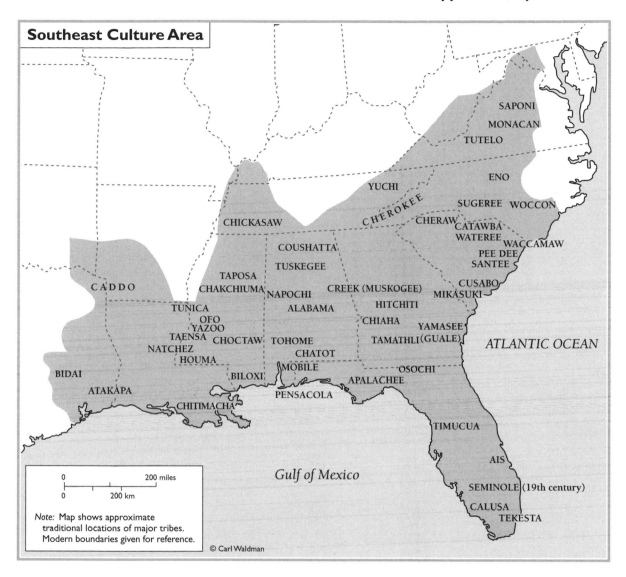

Southeast Culture Area

SAPONI
MONACAN
TUTELO

ENO

YUCHI

SUGEREE   WOCCON

CHEROKEE

CHICKASAW

CHERAW   CATAWBA
WATEREE
WACCAMAW
PEE DEE
SANTEE

COUSHATTA

TUSKEGEE

TAPOSA
CHAKCHIUMA   NAPOCHI   CREEK (MUSKOGEE)   CUSABO
MIKASUKI

CADDO

TUNICA   ALABAMA   HITCHITI

OFO
YAZOO   CHIAHA

TAENSA   CHOCTAW   TOHOME   TAMATHLI (GUALE)   YAMASEE

NATCHEZ   CHATOT   ATLANTIC OCEAN

HOUMA

BIDAI   MOBILE   OSOCHI

BILOXI   APALACHEE

ATAKAPA   PENSACOLA

CHITIMACHA

TIMUCUA

AIS

Gulf of Mexico

SEMINOLE (19th century)

CALUSA
TEKESTA

0 ————— 200 miles
0 ————— 200 km

Note: Map shows approximate
traditional locations of major tribes.
Modern boundaries given for reference.

© Carl Waldman

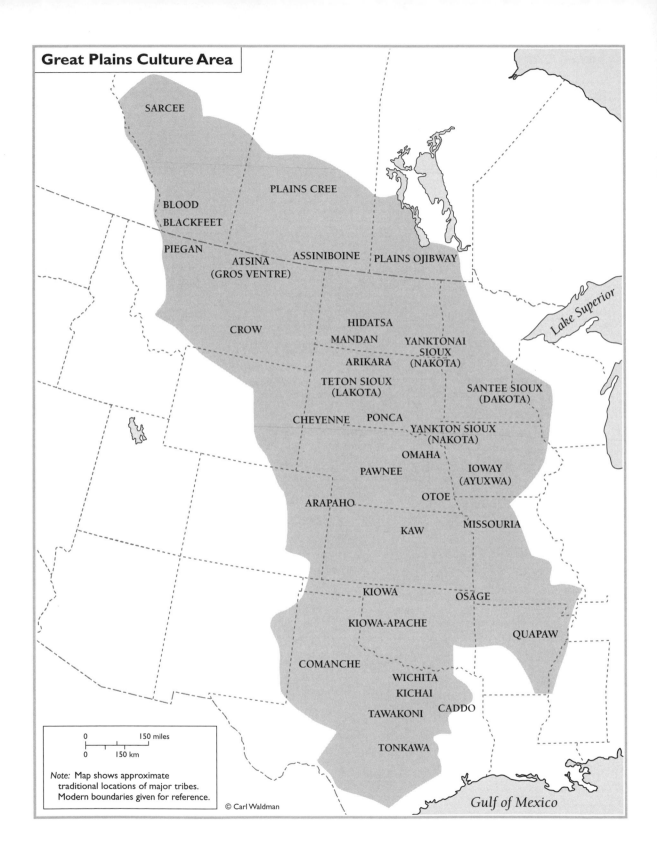

Great Plains Culture Area

SARCEE

PLAINS CREE

BLOOD
BLACKFEET
PIEGAN
ATSINA
(GROS VENTRE)
ASSINIBOINE
PLAINS OJIBWAY

Lake Superior

CROW

HIDATSA
MANDAN
YANKTONAI
SIOUX
(NAKOTA)
ARIKARA
TETON SIOUX
(LAKOTA)
SANTEE SIOUX
(DAKOTA)

CHEYENNE
PONCA
YANKTON SIOUX
(NAKOTA)
OMAHA
PAWNEE
IOWAY
(AYUXWA)
ARAPAHO
OTOE
KAW
MISSOURIA

KIOWA
OSAGE
KIOWA-APACHE
QUAPAW

COMANCHE
WICHITA
KICHAI
CADDO
TAWAKONI

TONKAWA

0   150 miles

0   150 km

Note: Map shows approximate
traditional locations of major tribes.
Modern boundaries given for reference.

© Carl Waldman

Gulf of Mexico

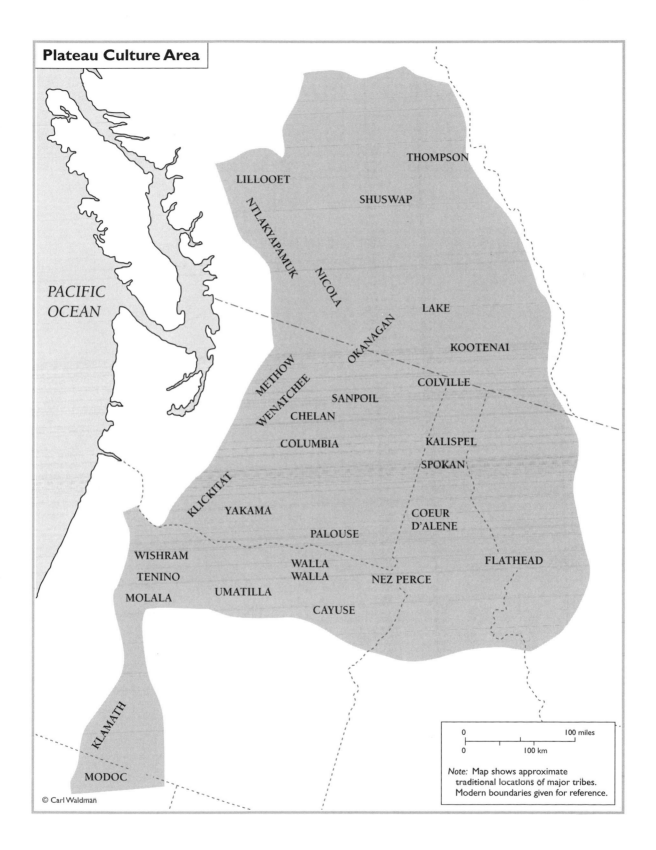

Plateau Culture Area

PACIFIC
OCEAN

THOMPSON

LILLOOET

SHUSWAP

NTLAKYAPAMUK

NICOLA

LAKE

OKANAGAN

KOOTENAI

METHOW

COLVILLE

WENATCHEE

SANPOIL

CHELAN

KALISPEL

COLUMBIA

SPOKAN

KLICKITAT

YAKAMA

COEUR
D'ALENE

PALOUSE

WISHRAM

WALLA
WALLA

FLATHEAD

TENINO

NEZ PERCE

MOLALA

UMATILLA

CAYUSE

KLAMATH

MODOC

© Carl Waldman

0		100 miles
0	100 km	

Note: Map shows approximate
traditional locations of major tribes.
Modern boundaries given for reference.

Great Basin Culture Area

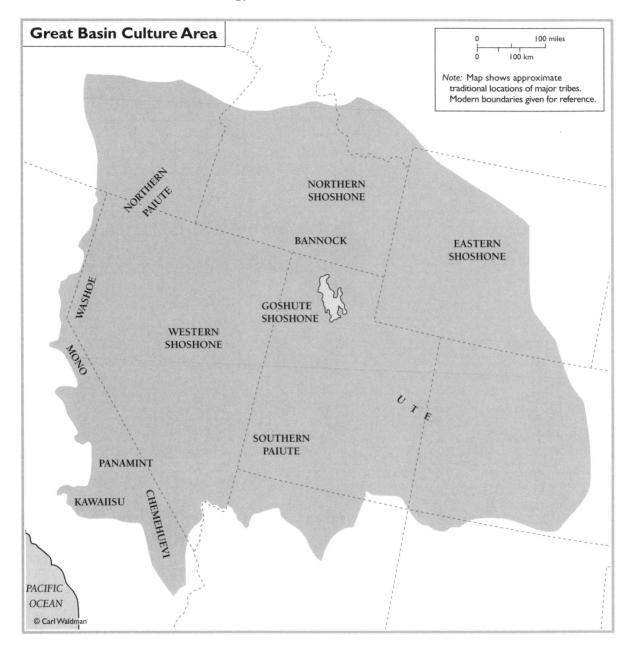

0 ____ 100 miles
0 ____ 100 km

Note: Map shows approximate
traditional locations of major tribes.
Modern boundaries given for reference.

NORTHERN PAIUTE

NORTHERN SHOSHONE

BANNOCK

EASTERN SHOSHONE

WASHOE

GOSHUTE SHOSHONE

MONO

WESTERN SHOSHONE

U T E

PANAMINT

SOUTHERN PAIUTE

KAWAIISU

CHEMEHUEVI

PACIFIC OCEAN

© Carl Waldman

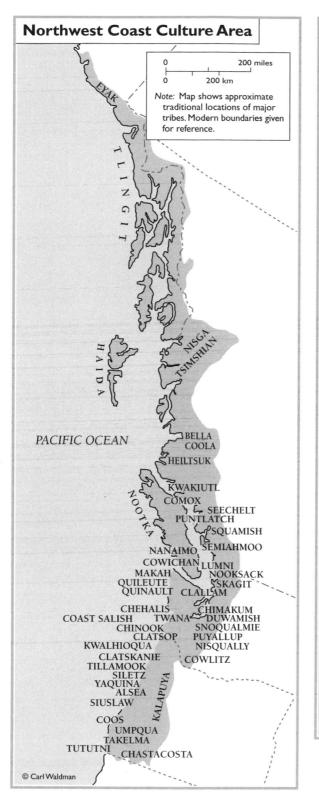

Northwest Coast Culture Area

EYAK

TLINGIT

HAIDA

NISGA
TSIMSHIAN

PACIFIC OCEAN

BELLA COOLA

HEILTSUK

KWAKIUTL
COMOX
SEECHELT
PUNTLATCH
SQUAMISH
NANAIMO
SEMIAHMOO
COWICHAN
LUMNI
NOOKSACK
MAKAH
SKAGIT
QUILEUTE
QUINAULT
CLALLAM
CHEHALIS
CHIMAKUM
COAST SALISH
TWANA
DUWAMISH
CHINOOK
SNOQUALMIE
CLATSOP
PUYALLUP
KWALHIOQUA
NISQUALLY
CLATSKANIE
COWLITZ
TILLAMOOK
SILETZ
YAQUINA
ALSEA
SIUSLAW
COOS
UMPQUA
TAKELMA
TUTUTNI
CHASTACOSTA
KALAPUYA
NOOTKA

0   200 miles
0   200 km

Note: Map shows approximate traditional locations of major tribes. Modern boundaries given for reference.

© Carl Waldman

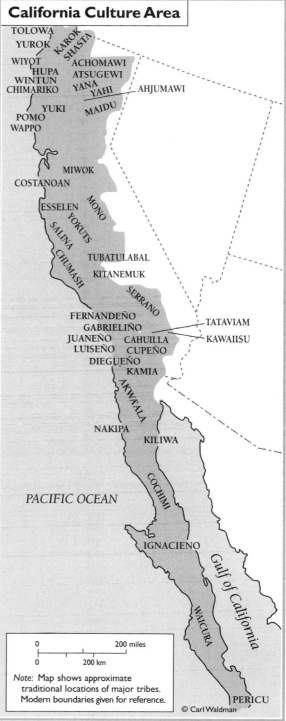

California Culture Area

TOLOWA
YUROK
KAROK
SHASTA
WIYOT
ACHOMAWI
HUPA
ATSUGEWI
WINTUN
YANA
CHIMARIKO
YAHI
AHJUMAWI
YUKI
MAIDU
POMO
WAPPO
MIWOK
COSTANOAN
ESSELEN
MONO
YOKUTS
SALINA
CHUMASH
TUBATULABAL
KITANEMUK
SERRANO
FERNANDEÑO
TATAVIAM
GABRIELIÑO
KAWAIISU
JUANEÑO
CAHUILLA
LUISEÑO
CUPEÑO
DIEGUEÑO
KAMIA
AKWAALA
NAKIPA
KILIWA

PACIFIC OCEAN

COCHIMI
IGNACIENO

WAICURA

Gulf of California

0   200 miles
0   200 km

Note: Map shows approximate traditional locations of major tribes. Modern boundaries given for reference.

PERICU

© Carl Waldman

Southwest Culture Area

HUALAPAI
HAVASUPAI
HOPI
MOJAVE
NAVAJO
JICARILLA
APACHE
HALCHIDHOMA
YAVAPAI
TIWA
MARICOPA
TOWA
TEWA
ZUNI
PECOS
YUMA
KERES
COCOPAH
PIRO
TIWA
WESTERN
APACHE
MIMBRENO
APACHE
TOHONO
O'ODHAM
CHIRICAHUA
APACHE
MESCALERO
APACHE
AKIMEL
O'ODHAM
SUMA
OPATA
JUMANO
SERI
CAHITA
JOVA
CONCHO
YAQUI
TARAHUMARA
LIPAN
APACHE
TEPAHUE
KARANKAWA
VAVROHIO
TOBOSO
MAYO
ZOE
COMANITO
NIO
COAHUILTEC
LAGUNERO
GUASAVE
TEPEHUAN
ZACATEC
BOCALOS
JANAMBRE
PISONES
NEGRITO
TAMAULIPEC
HUICHOL
TEPECANO
GUACHICHIL
GUAMARES
JONAZ
COLOTLAN
TEUL
PAME

Gulf of California

PACIFIC OCEAN

Gulf of Mexico

0   150 miles
0   150 km

Note: Map shows approximate
traditional locations of major tribes.
Modern boundaries given for reference.

© Carl Waldman

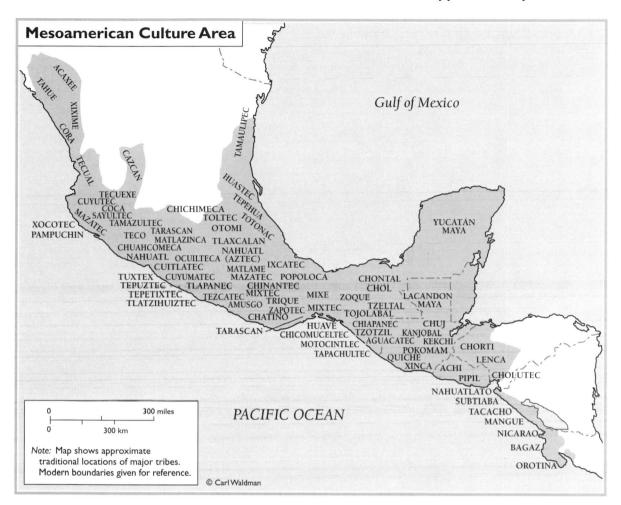

Mesoamerican Culture Area

ACAXEE
TAHUE
XIXIME
CORA
TECUAL
CAZCAN

TAMAULIPEC

Gulf of Mexico

HUASTEC
TEPEHUA
TECUEXE
CUYUTEC
COCA
SAYULTEC
TAMAZULTEC
XOCOTEC
MAZATEC
TECO
CHUAHCOMECA
NAHUATL
NAHUATL OCUILTECA
CUITLATEC
TUXTEX
CUYUMATEC
TEPUZTEC
TLAPANEC
TEPETIXTEC
TEZCATEC
TLATZIHUIZTEC
AMUSGO

CHICHIMECA
TOLTEC
TOTONAC
OTOMI
TARASCAN
MATLAZINCA
TLAXCALAN
MATLAME
(AZTEC)
MATLAME
IXCATEC
MAZATEC POPOLOCA
CHINANTEC
MIXTEC
TRIQUE
ZAPOTEC
CHATINO

MIXE
MIXTEC

YUCATÁN
MAYA

CHONTAL
CHOL

ZOQUE
LACANDON
TZELTAL MAYA
TOJOLABAL

TARASCAN

CHICOMUCELTEC
MOTOCINTLEC
TAPACHULTEC

HUAVE
TZOTZIL
AGUACATEC
QUICHE
XINCA
ACHI

CHIAPANEC
KANJOBAL
KEKCHI
POKOMAM
CHUJ

CHORTI
LENCA

PIPIL
CHOLUTEC
NAHUATLATO
SUBTIABA
TACACHO
MANGUE
NICARAO
BAGAZ
OROTINA

PACIFIC OCEAN

0   300 miles
0   300 km

Note: Map shows approximate
traditional locations of major tribes.
Modern boundaries given for reference.

© Carl Waldman

Circum-Caribbean Culture Area

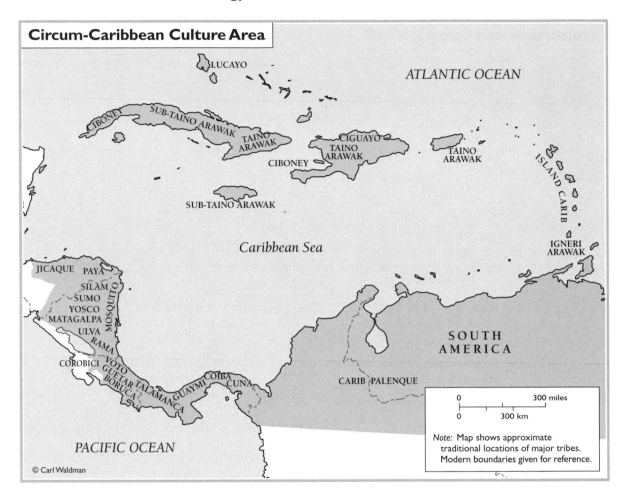

South American Culture Areas

CIRCUM-CARIBBEAN

CARIB
PALENQUE

TUPI
ARAWAK

AGUARUNA
ACHUARI
JIVARO

CARIB

ARAWAK

TUPI

CHIMU

INCA

TROPICAL FOREST

ANDEAN

EASTERN
HIGHLANDS

GUARANI

GUARANI

CENTRAL AND SOUTHERN

MAPUCHE

PAMPAS

TIERRA DEL FUEGO

ANDEAN   Culture areas

PAMPAS   Regions

MAPUCHE   Tribes and peoples

———   Approximate culture
          area boundaries

- - - -   Approximate regional
          boundaries

0   800 miles

0   800 km

Note: See the Circum-Caribbean map
for the entire scope of the culture area.

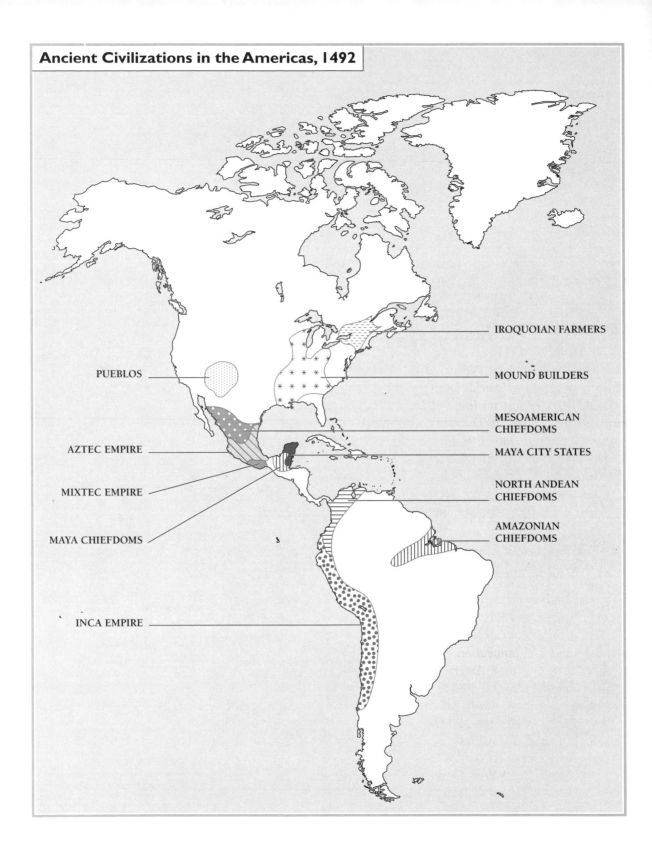

Ancient Civilizations in the Americas, 1492

IROQUOIAN FARMERS

PUEBLOS

MOUND BUILDERS

MESOAMERICAN
CHIEFDOMS

AZTEC EMPIRE

MAYA CITY STATES

MIXTEC EMPIRE

NORTH ANDEAN
CHIEFDOMS

AMAZONIAN
CHIEFDOMS

MAYA CHIEFDOMS

INCA EMPIRE

FURTHER READING

Books

Baquedano, Elizabeth. *Aztec, Inca and Maya.* New York: DK Publishing, 2000.

Bol, Marsha C., editor. *North, South, East, West: American Indians in the Natural World.* Lanham, Md.: Roberts Rinehart, 1998.

Brown, Fern. *American Indian Science.* New York: Twenty-first Century Books, 1997.

Carrasco, David. *Daily Life of the Aztecs: Keepers of the Sun and Moon.* Westport, Conn.: Greenwood Press, 1998.

Cajete, Gregory. *American Indian Science: Natural Laws of Interdependence.* Santa Fe, N. Mex.: Clear Light Publications, 1999.

———. *A Peoples' Ecology.* Santa Fe, N. Mex.: Clear Light Books, 1999.

Goodchild, Peter. *Survival Skills of the North American Indians.* 2d ed. Chicago: Chicago Review Press, 1999.

Hawke, Sharryl Davis, and James E. Davis. *Seeds of Change: The Story of Cultural Exchange after 1492.* New York: Addison-Wesley, 1993.

Keoke, Emory, and Kay Marie Porterfield. *The Encyclopedia of American Indian Contributions to the World: 15,000 Years of Inventions and Innovation.* New York: Facts On File, 2002.

Liptak, Karen. *North American Indian Survival Skills.* New York: Franklin Watts, 1990.

Malpass, Micahel A. *Daily Life in the Inca Empire.* Westport, Conn.: Greenwood Press, 2002.

Murdoch, David. *Eyewitness: North American Indians.* New York: DK Publishers, 2000.

Petty, Carolyn A. *Water Drum Science: Science through American Indian Art and Culture.* Chino Valley, Ariz.: Creative Education Consulting, 1996.

Sharer, Robert J. *Daily Life in Maya Civilization.* Westport, Conn.: Greenwood Press, 2002.

Steedman, Scott. *How Would You Survive As an American Indian?* New York: Franklin Watts, 1997.

Wood, Marian. *Ancient America: Cultural Atlas for Young People,* rev. ed. New York: Facts On File, 2003.

Young, Biloine Whiting, and Richard Fowler. *Cahokia: The Great Native American Metropolis.* Urbana: University of Illinois Press, 1999.

Other Resources

The American Indian Science and Engineering Society (AISES) works to combine science with traditional American Indian values. This organization provides educational programs for American Indian and Alaskan students from kindergarten to college. Its Web site (http://www.aises.org) gives information about the programs that the organization sponsors.

The Society for Advancement of Chicanos and Native Americans in Science (SACNAS) is an organization that encourages Chicano/Latino and Native American students to pursue graduate degrees in science. Its Web site (http://www.sacnas.org) contains many biographies of contemporary Chicano/Latino and American Indian scientists written for high school and middle school students.

INDEX

Page numbers in *italic* indicate photographs. Page numbers in **boldface** indicate box features. Page numbers followed by *m* indicate maps. Page numbers followed by *g* indicate glossary entries. Page numbers followed by *t* indicate time line entries.

10-08